teach yourself®

baby signing

baby signing
jane jarvis

Launched in 1938, the **teach yourself** series grew rapidly in response to the world's wartime needs. Loved and trusted by over 50 million readers, the series has continued to respond to society's changing interests and passions and now, 70 years on, includes over 500 titles, from Arabic and Beekeeping to Yoga and Zulu. What would you like to learn?

be where you want to be with **teach yourself**

For UK order enquiries: please contact Bookpoint Ltd, 130 Milton Park, Abingdon, Oxon OX14 4SB. Telephone: +44 (0) 1235 827720. Fax: +44 (0) 1235 400454. Lines are open 09.00–17.00, Monday to Saturday, with a 24-hour message answering service. Details about our titles and how to order are available at www.teachyourself.co.uk

Long renowned as the authoritative source for self-guided learning – with more than 50 million copies sold worldwide – the **teach yourself** series includes over 500 titles in the fields of languages, crafts, hobbies, business, computing and education.

British Library Cataloguing in Publication Data: a catalogue record for this title is available from the British Library.

First published in UK 2008 by Hodder Education, part of Hachette Livre UK, 338 Euston Road, London, NW1 3BH.

This edition published 2008.

The **teach yourself** name is a registered trade mark of Hodder Headline.

Copyright © 2008 Jane Jarvis

Typeset by Transet Limited, Coventry, England.
Printed in Great Britain for Hodder Education, an Hachette Livre UK Company, 338 Euston Road, London NW1 3BH, by Cox & Wyman Ltd, Reading, Berkshire.

The publisher has used its best endeavours to ensure that the URLs for external websites referred to in this book are correct and active at the time of going to press. However, the publisher and the author have no responsibility for the websites and can make no guarantee that a site will remain live or that the content will remain relevant, decent or appropriate.

Hachette Livre UK's policy is to use papers that are natural, renewable and recyclable products and made from wood grown in sustainable forests. The logging and manufacturing processes are expected to conform to the environmental regulations of the country of origin.

Impression number	10 9 8 7 6 5 4 3 2 1
Year	2012 2011 2010 2009 2008

contents

acknowledgements

I would like to take this opportunity to express my sincere, heartfelt thanks firstly to Sasha Felix, Director of Sing and Sign. Without her vision and leadership, Sing and Sign wouldn't be what it is today. Sasha not only inspired me to begin signing with my own children, but to begin teaching parents how to sign with their own babies. Later on I joined Sasha in the office, co-ordinating the local franchise area and liaising with the many franchisees, all of whom wanted to share the wonders of baby signing with other parents. My time with Sing and Sign was wonderful, and I truly miss them since my move to Australia.

I would also like to thank my wonderful husband for giving me the space to write this book and taking on extra childcare duties (and I *so* wanted to say extra cleaning duties too!). This book began while working within the Sing and Sign family in UK, but finished with just the four of us, following a huge international move. Your love and support during this time has been invaluable.

This book also wouldn't have been possible without the support of my parents and my in-laws, who at different times have either offered me the quietness of their house, or helped with childcare to enable me to finish this project – a huge THANK YOU to you.

This book wouldn't be complete without fantastic parents, who have been passionate about signing with their children, and wanted to share their story. Thank you to all who contributed, whether your story made it to final publication or not.

This book was also helped my wonderful friends who proof-read, gave expert medical advice and general help and encouragement. Most of you asked not to be named – but you know who you are – and I love you all!

introduction

This book will teach you how to:

- understand the principles of baby signing
- know the benefits of signing with your baby
- begin signing with your baby
- introduce signs that are relevant to your baby's world
- be aware of any special needs and what action to take
- continue using appropriate signs with older children.

People have been signing with their babies for years; in fact, it is so natural that most of us already use signs and gestures with our babies without realizing it! The most common reason for doing so is an intense desire on the part of a parent to find out exactly what is going on in a baby's mind – what do they need? What do they want? What do they think about and remember? All parents want what is best for their children, and one of the fundamental ways to nurture and understand a child is by good communication.

Babies often have more intelligence then we give them credit for, purely because they have limited means to let us know what their thoughts and needs are. Their undeveloped vocal cords restrict them from fully participating in the verbal language around them, and in fact most babies' vocal cords must develop for 16 months or so before they can pronounce clear words. However, the good news is that babies develop the fine muscles in their hands long before they develop those muscles required for speech, so they're equipped to communicate with you long before they can speak! Baby signing can help parents, carers and all of those important people in a child's world to understand them, interact with them, and most importantly to have lots of fun.

This book aims not only to inspire and help you to introduce signing with your child, it also practically shows you many signs that are useful for you and your baby. You will find references and illustrations to over 100 signs within the book, and many more on the accompanying DVD.

01

history and principles of baby signing

In this chapter you will learn:
- what baby signing is and how it all began
- how signing is beneficial to your baby's development
- the Sing and Sign approach to baby signing.

Early communication

To understand baby signing, it can be helpful to go back and think through the earliest forms of communication we can have with our baby.

Even from within the womb, babies are trying to communicate. You may be surprised to discover parents have recorded 'communicating' or 'playing' with their unborn babies in the womb. By pressing or rubbing one side of the mother's stomach, an unborn baby may respond to the touch with a kick or an elbow; by repeating it on the other side, parents can 'play' and communicate with their unborn baby. Babies also respond to loud music and even their parents' singing. All of these are the earliest forms of communication. The awareness of speech sounds is also developing during this time in the womb. Researchers have discovered that an unborn baby's heart rate will decrease at the sound of their mother's voice. Having continual communication is important with babies and children. By reading stories, singing, and talking to your baby, even in the womb, parents can help to promote developing language skills.

From birth until about 4 months of age, babies' principal communication consists mainly of reflexive crying to express feelings of hunger, tiredness, boredom or pain. Much of their communication will be through facial expressions and the movements of their arms, legs and fingers. They will also use smiling, cooing and other sounds of pleasure to communicate needs and feelings. Mirroring sounds and early words, responding to their communication and answering your baby's cries, are all ways to start your baby on the road to speech.

Liz Attenborough, manager of the Talk To Your Baby campaign, said:

'The level of interaction between young children and adults has a significant impact on their communication skills later in life.

Studies on Romanian orphans who received little contact with adults in their early life have found that they have language problems for the rest of their lives.

Babies are born without all their neurological pathways connected, so their interactions during the first few months and years of life play an important part in how they develop.'

The next stage of communication is what has been referred to as 'babbling'. At the age of around 4–6 months, babies start to make many more sounds including vowel sounds. Before speaking words, babies practise the sounds, intonations and rhythms of language, as well as extensive body language and facial expressions to communicate. Interestingly, babies will often babble more when they are alone. Through interaction with you, babies mirror and learn early language skills. Many parents will find they adjust their speech and use 'motherease' or 'baby-talk', trying hard to interpret unintelligible utterances! This helps to socialize children with simplified language and introduces them gradually to adult language.

Between 6–12 months, most babies are beginning to use a combination of gestures and sounds to make themselves understood. This is a charming but very frustrating stage of their development. From around 6 months, babies begin to *reach* for objects: babies love 'peek-a-boo' and will show willingness to continue the game on and on, by reaching towards your hand or whatever you are using to hide behind. Words begin to have some meaning but this will be very context dependent. During this time, babies begin to respond to some simple requests such as 'up you come'. At around 9 months, communication becomes increasingly *intentional*: your baby may give/show an object as a way to communicate, which paves the way for pointing. They begin to understand names of familiar objects and people. Your baby's babbling may begin to be produced in longer strings ('bababa mamama'). Your baby will often point at things, shake their head for 'no' and wave. These are symbolic gestures that are one form of communication used by pre-verbal babies and toddlers. In addition to pointing and grunting, and trying to 'sing' to music, your baby has the potential use of their hands and body to aid in communicating their thoughts, wants, fears, needs and memories. At this point, they are beginning to understand a lot about themselves and their world, but for most babies they are still lacking a precise way to express their thoughts and needs.

The first single words spoken (usually a child's version of the adult word, e.g. 'du' for 'duck') occurs usually at around 12 months. You will notice your baby will understand names of people and objects if they are in their usual context. At this stage, babies often use lots of gestures to express meaning, as their understanding is typically in advance of actual spoken language. They will often invent 'signs' to convey their meaning (arms to be lifted up etc.).

By around 14–20 months of age, a child will usually begin to combine their gestures with actual words. They begin with simple words that they will have heard often, such as 'mama' or 'dada'. These words eventually turn into two-word phrases, which is the next step on the journey of speech. Two-word phrases, such as 'shoes on', 'doggie gone', or 'Daddy home', begin around the age of 2 years. However, this is a very long time in your baby's fast developing world to wait to be fully understood. Using signs and gestures gives babies a way to effectively 'talk' with their parents, long before they can use speech to communicate. It is more effective and precise than cooing, crying, smiling, grunting or flapping their hands, and eliminates much of the guesswork associated with a young child. Babies can, and do communicate about the world around them, long before they have mastered their verbal speaking skills.

(Please note: The ages shown are merely a guide – it's important to note that, like other aspects of development, the process of acquiring language is gradual and varies greatly between children).

What *is* baby signing?

Baby signing is really very easy. It doesn't need too much explanation; baby signing is, in essence, simple hand gestures. Signing is so natural that you are probably already 'signing' to your baby without realizing it! Think about it – most of us will wave goodbye to babies happily and comfortably all the time without even thinking much about it. We all know this helps them start to understand what 'goodbye' means, and that when they wave back to us they are well on their way to *saying* 'bye-bye' too. This is, in reality, a baby's first 'sign'.

Throughout this book you will find many examples and case studies of parents signing with their children to give you confidence and inspire you in your own baby-signing journey. Parents have often said how helpful it is to hear other stories, not only as an encouragement, but also to suggest creative ways of using signing that they may not have thought of.

Most children will point, wave and learn to nod and shake their heads. Baby signing classes, and this book, aim to help and encourage parents to use a few more gestures or 'signs' for other important and relevant words in your baby's world. It isn't necessary to learn a whole dictionary of sign language.

Baby signing will help you, to help your baby understand sooner, and effectively communicate with you earlier and more successfully during the long process of learning to talk!

Parents can sometimes think signing with their baby is harder and more complicated than it is, not realizing that it is an extension of natural communication.

I had no idea how easy signing was with your baby – I was a little sceptical at first. We learnt many of the signs through songs – which really helped. Also a lot of the signs mimic an activity or movement, or represent a shape of an object so they are easily remembered. The wider family have easily been effectively communicating with my son, and the difference is amazing.

Martin, dad of Josiah

How baby signing began

The most significant research and interest in baby sign language began in the early 1980s by two separate and convincing research projects, although sign language itself has records dating as far back as the 16th century. One project was undertaken by Joseph Garcia – a student at Alaska Pacific University – and, at a concomitant time, a ground breaking 20-year study was undertaken by pioneers in the field: Linda Acredolo, Ph.D and Susan Goodwyn, Ph.D, both from the University of California, Davis. Both research projects began due to the inspiration of the researchers' own children.

As baby signing is still an emerging phenomenon, especially within the UK, all research that has been undertaken in this area is absolutely vital and important to document. It is therefore helpful to understand some of the roots from where baby signing emerged. However, if you are really keen to move straight onto the mechanics and practical instruction on how to begin signing with your baby, then you may wish to move directly to Chapter 02, and come back to read this section later.

During the 1970s, Garcia worked as an interpreter and became fascinated with his observations that babies of his deaf friends were quickly becoming sign language 'experts' around the age of 9 months. In the same way, his studies also showed babies of hearing parents were not communicating much at this same point in their development. In 1987, while attending Alaska Pacific University, Garcia began to research the use of American Sign Language for hearing babies of hearing parents, and the effect this would have on their communication.

Garcia's own infant sons were a great advantage in his research, and became 'test subjects' for what eventually developed into his 'Sign With Your Baby' and 'Sign 2 Me' programmes based on American Sign Language (ASL).

During the same time, Linda Acredolo had observed her daughter Katie watching the fish swimming in the fish tank at the paediatrician's office. Katie walked up to the tank to take a closer look and started to blow. Her mother became puzzled at the behaviour. Once they were home, Katie was put down for a nap in her cot. Above the cot hung a beautiful fish mobile, Linda leaned in to set in motion the mobile with a gentle blow. It was at that point Linda remembered her daughter in the paediatrician's office and immediately made the connection of Katie 'communicating' with the fish earlier that day.

Over two decades, Acredolo, her research partner Goodwyn, and their team began to study the impact of signing with babies as compared to those babies who did not sign. They were funded by a grant from the National Institutes of Child Health and Human Development, USA and they were able to identify the progress of children at ages 2, 3 and 8 years old.

This amazing 20-year study was devised to look at 'how baby signing affected children's linguistic and intellectual development'. The study began by comparing three groups of 11-month-olds:

Group One: Parents were asked to encourage baby signing (alongside speech) when interacting.

Group Two: Parents were to focus on naming things (verbally) for their baby.

Group Three: Parents had no specific instruction at all.

The babies underwent a language assessment at regular intervals up to the age of 3 and were followed up again at age 8. Their initial results were amazing and made compelling reading. The tests showed that the baby signers' language skills (Group One) were in advance of the non-signers and that they spoke in sentences earlier. At 3 years of age, the baby signers had language skills normally expected of 4 year-olds. At age 8, the children who had used baby signs scored significantly higher on the IQ test than the non-signers.

Acredolo and Goodwyn continued with their research and provided psychology scholars with interesting results. Two decades of research results proved signers out-performed non-signers in many areas of cognition and language development. **They concluded that using baby signs improves language and cognitive ability and, furthermore, that this did not end when babies started to talk, and that in fact using baby signing has far reaching implications long after the child has stopped using the signs.**

The results of Acredolo and Goodwyn's work formed the basis of their book and programme 'Baby Signs'. The book is based on a concept which allows babies to create their own signs to communicate in order to bridge the gap between cognition and communication. They primarily recommend that parents invent signs to use with their babies, not necessarily following any formal system. This approach can be valuable as parents are inspired to constantly be on the lookout for things their baby is interested in and invent signs accordingly, which would be relevant to their child's own interests. However, a parent would have to be highly motivated and resourceful to invent, remember and stick to a set of signs they themselves have created and which no-one else understands.

Linda Acredolo, Ph.D, is a Professor Emeritus of Psychology at the University of California, Davis. Susan Goodwyn, Ph.D, is a Professor of Psychology and Child Development at California State University, Stanislaus. Both researchers live and work in Northern California. Without the statistical research from Acredolo and Goodwyn, we may not be aware of the positive impact that the introduction of sign language has to a baby's cognitive and language development.

From this significant research study and sign language programmes, many grass root baby sign language programmes have emerged from America. Many of the current programmes are based on ASL (American Sign Language) and facilitate verbal development as an end result goal.

Clearly then, the research shows that gesture is a very natural part of language development and helps communication skills develop. Communication through speech is the essence of being human; it's what distinguishes us from the animal world. Using extra specific gestures (or baby signs) can improve language skills and help babies both with understanding and talking as well as providing both parents and babies with a rich, rewarding first experience of communication.

> *My interest in baby signing was raised by a friend who described watching a family signing together. As someone who uses BSL (British Sign Language), she approached the family to ask more about the child who was signing. They explained that they were using baby sign language and how useful it had been. They described how it helped ease frustration and enabled communication of important issues such as pain and hunger. I decided that this was worth investigating!*
>
> Jo and Jess from Bristol

The benefits of baby signing

The rewards of signing with your baby are potentially very significant. As we have already discovered in the section on the history of baby signing, research has shown us many of the benefits of signing with your baby. However, there is still interesting ongoing research into the effect of baby signing on the development of a baby's brain. In the earliest years of life, babies' brains are 'wiring' themselves through their experiences. While using signs, parents say accompanying words and tend to give increased language input, giving your child the opportunity of a greater understanding of words concepts. For example, you may see a cat and say to your baby, 'Do you see the cat? Look he's high up there in the tree. He's a lovely big, black cat. I wonder how high he can climb?' etc. Instantly you have talked about something that is of interest, instinctively given more information, and very naturally enhanced the word 'cat' whilst your baby is hearing more spoken words, different ideas and concepts in a very natural and relaxed way.

> *Signing has allowed us to understand each other from very early on; I feel that he started telling me what interests him, what he does and doesn't want to do and what's going on in 'his world' months before he was able to talk. I'm sure our ability to communicate through signs has not only strengthened our bond, but also helps us avoid too many tantrums!*
>
> Jane Kirkby with her son Ben

Signing babies can communicate complex things earlier. Many experts suggest this stimulates brain development and enhances the building of brain circuitry.

> In her fascinating book, *Dancing With Words, Signing for Hearing Children's Literacy*, Professor Marilyn Daniels of Pennsylvania State University writes:
>
> *'Sign language instruction, with its requisite visual component creates an increase in brain activity by engaging the visual cortex and presenting an additional language to the young learner. The heightened cerebral action occurs in both the right and left hemispheres of the brain. This increase in language activity stimulates the development of the brain by stimulating the formation of more synapses, or connections among brain cells. The brains of children up to about the age of eight continue to develop and grow in this manner in response to environmental input. Brain cells literally live or die as language experiences impinge upon them. Using sign language and English in tandem provides a much richer language base for brain activity and brain growth and development.*

Professor Daniels also likens signing to 'making pictures in the air' – an incredibly useful tool when trying to give meaning to words that are abstract or concepts that are difficult for your baby to understand. You may find telling your child to put their coat on because it is 'cold' outside, or their hat on because it is windy, are actually difficult concepts for them to understand, as they can't *see* the cold or the wind. A bag of frozen peas can help illustrate the 'cold' sign, and you may find it then becomes one they use quite quickly! Using signs and gestures – making words visual – can often make a difficult concept easily understood by your baby.

'Signing' has been a brilliant asset for us as Rosie has been able to avoid the whole phase of frustration that comes before they can talk. The signing started to come out just as Rosie got seriously ill for the first time with chicken pox and she was able to tell me exactly what she wanted. It has always been taught so functionally, it is really useful and relevant to her daily activities. It has helped us to get through struggles with nappy changes, boredom in cars and lots more. Now Rosie is able to talk we still keep on going as she continues to learn new signs, she loves all the music and the signs remain incredibly helpful when I need to communicate to her across a noisy room. I would highly recommend signing to anyone and intend to do it with all my children.

Rachel

As we have already covered many of the benefits of signing with your baby, here are just a few edited highlights!

What baby signing allows babies to enjoy

- Communication that would otherwise not be possible.
- Enhanced early vocabulary and understanding.
- Increased confidence from being more readily understood.
- An above-average ability later in life to learn a new language.
- Reduced frustration levels (for parent and baby).

What baby signing helps parents to do

- Stimulate a baby's intellectual and emotional development.
- Enrich baby's relationships.
- Share a deeper bond with your baby because you have greater insight into their mind, thoughts, needs and ideas.
- Obtain a higher level of trust from your baby because he or she knows that you understand what they are trying to tell you.
- Gain satisfaction. What a great feeling it is to know that you can effectively communicate with your pre-verbal infant.
- Encourage the development of speech.

> *In the past year, there have been so many times that I was thankful for us learning to sign, it's been so useful in hundreds of situations and also great fun for both of us.*
>
> Laura and Luke

So what about British baby signing?

Across the UK, there are now many signing programmes available to parents. However, after much research and for the purposes of this book, we are focusing on the Sing and Sign approach to baby signing.

Sing and Sign was the first British baby signing programme and its original and unique approach has revolutionized baby signing in the UK. The programme was devised by the mother and musician Sasha Felix, and developed with the help of speech and language professionals, launching in January 2001. The programme began with local classes, but such was the interest that a DVD was launched later on that year which has since taught thousands of parents across the world how to sign with their babies and encourage early communication.

Such was the impact that Sing and Sign made in the UK, especially initially in the South East where it was launched, that within three years Sure Start was recommending it. Sure Start is the government-backed service working to promote all aspects of development in babies and young children.

> *Sing and Sign is a brilliant programme. We suggest all our mums and babies use signs, as gesture is a natural first form of communication. The gestures shown in Sing and Sign can help babies understand more of what is said to them and enables babies to express themselves earlier. Using signs can make life for parents far less stressful!*
>
> Susan Duffy, Speech and Language Therapist for Sure Start

Obviously with such positive research initially coming through from the United States, and the myths (see FAQ's in Chapter 08) surrounding teaching babies how to sign before speech slowly being eradicated, the press soon took hold of the baby signing phenomenon and it wasn't long before many other baby signing programmes began to develop – especially within the UK. Some programmes began as evening classes promoting teaching parents and adults basic signs to use with their babies, other programmes would teach British Sign Language (see further information in Chapter 08, page 153), whilst many others would be a parent and child type setting focusing primarily on signing with your own child. It would be impossible to try and adequately cover every baby-signing programme that is currently available to parents within the UK at the present time. For that reason, and after much research, we will be proceeding with just one programme that will hopefully help, encourage and inspire you and therefore be the most beneficial way forward in beginning your own baby-signing journey. The last part of this chapter will outline the Sing and Sign approach to baby signing which will help you understand the methodology behind the teaching in the rest of the book.

Everyone knows that nursery rhymes and action songs are really enjoyable for babies and children, and musical activities help stimulate language development. In slightly older children, doing things rhythmically begins to get children moving in a way that persuasion and even bribery cannot. Sing and Sign is unique in the fact that it so effectively combines the benefits of both music *and* baby signing.

The research literature on music enrichment for infants and toddlers has been prolific. We know that music participation teaches music skills, perception, and cognition. Simultaneously it also promotes child development areas such as listening skills, language development, motor coordination, cooperative social skills and reciprocity … demonstrating the power of music to be a highly beneficial reinforcer for children from the moment of their birth.

Jayne Standley, Ph.D

The Sing and Sign approach to teaching baby signing

The aim of Sing and Sign is for babies to enjoy the musical and social aspect of classes while their parents learn about baby signing. The programme aims to tap into a baby's highly gestural phase of their life and, using a thorough and well-developed format, take them forward right through until they are mastering speech.

Sign and Sign teaches a wide range of signs using some traditional and some specially written or adapted songs in a fun and relaxed way. What makes the programme special is that every sign used in a song relates to those important first words of a baby's world: nappies and bath time; hiding games and bedtime; going to the park, and other things that capture a child's imagination like animals and vehicles. You name it, the programme has a song about it, and the babies just love to hear them!

Teach Yourself Baby Signing aims to follow the curriculum of the course as much as possible within the confines of a book. We will use the same guidelines that are presented in class, as well as following some of the order and routines of topics that you will find on the course. These can be found primarily in Chapters 02, 03 and 04. The course is full of songs and rhymes, whereas this book is only able to offer a few ideas to enable you

---

I took Natasha and her older sister out in the car. In my mirror I saw her signing the beginning of the song 'wind the bobbin up', so we ended up singing it to her about 30 times – she was very happy!

Melanie Warren

---

to sing your way through routines.

The curriculum is designed with the aim not only to give you the parent continuity of learning the signs, but to give the added aspect of routine for the babies – and we know how much babies love routine. On the course, songs, puppets, props, pictures and instruments are used to help inspire your baby's interest and facilitate in illustrating the signs. Using this book at home you can be inventive with how to present the signs to your baby. Throughout this book you will also find many examples of straightforward ways in which to introduce the signs to your baby, as well as integrating them into your daily living. The signs are separated into basic signs and secondary signs.

Basic signs

These signs are those which will be appropriate to all babies and cover familiar daily routines. Parents are first encouraged to use the routine basic signs with confidence, introducing more on a weekly basis. In class particular basic signs are highlighted as 'Signs of the Week' for parents to begin using at home. By participating in Sing and Sign groups at Stage One, parents become familiar with 80+ basic signs. Alongside this instruction, parents are also shown many potentially motivating secondary signs.

Secondary signs

These signs cover animals, vehicles, toys etc. which, although shown in class, are more usually used away from class and when baby is ready. From the wide variety of secondary signs covered in Sing and Sign Stage One, parents can use those which best suit their babies' interests. Once a baby begins to communicate interest in things by pointing, then more secondary signs can be shown.

You will find both basic and secondary signs are covered within

> We started signing with Tahlia when she was 7 months old, using a book. We've been taking her to Sing and Sign classes since she was 9 months old and they've become her favourite activity of the week. She kicks her legs with excitement when I tell her where we're going. We use lots of the most relevant signs for her daily routine and animal signs for the books we read to her and the songs we sing at home. We sing to her a lot and the songs we've learnt from the classes are real favourites in our household.
>
> Alison

this book, enabling you to show your child a wide variety of signs to help stimulate their interest and encourage communication.

All the songs are signed, but don't worry, there aren't so many signs within the songs that you feel overwhelmed, just enough to highlight the key words. Many of the tunes used are traditional and familiar melodies, which ensures all songs are easy to sign along with for the beginner. Within this book we have used only the most traditional tunes with adjusted lyrics to enable you to easily incorporate signing and singing as part of your daily routine.

Sing and Sign is a simple format that grows with your child. Stage One is for babies of around 6–7 months of age and focuses on the basic and some secondary signs. Stage Two is aimed at babies/toddlers aged around 14 months+ and again, the programme is ideal for their stage of development, taking in concepts such as foods, weather and opposites, as well as enjoying topics such as colours, basic counting and phonics. By this time, many older babies are starting to use some words as well as continuing to sign more difficult words. *Teach Yourself Baby Signing* encompasses topics from both Stage One and Two of the curriculum, covering signs that will be beneficial for the pre-verbal baby, and those with emerging speech. We would recommend, whatever the age of your child, starting at Chapter 02, which uses the basic signs, following through Chapter 03, 04 and 05. The signs shown in Chapter 07 are more appropriate for babies aged 14 months+, focusing on the older child, using more difficult concepts and the use of phonics.

As we have discovered, babies have gained great understanding in learning most of what you say to them, but their vocabulary is still continuing to develop. If your child is experiencing any developmental delay or problems with hearing or speech, then Chapter 06 will be particularly important as it illustrates many of the more common difficulties and special needs associated with poor or delayed communication.

As the content and programme of Sing and Sign has been proved to be so effective, during the course of this book we will be using some of the material and signs used with kind permission of Sasha Felix, Founder and Director of Sing and Sign.

Some parents, although hearing about the benefits of signing with babies, still feel they need convincing that it would actually be good for their child. Parents often choose to join a baby class not only for the fun and social aspect of a class, but also for the educational or learning opportunities that can be achieved. Baby signing not only has excellent learning opportunities, it also adds an extra dimension to your life together, as your child learns words at an earlier age than you may have expected and gives you more opportunity to bond.

02

the early basics, getting started and basic guidelines

In this chapter you will learn:
- when it is appropriate to start signing with your baby
- how to begin signing and identifying your baby's signs
- recommended initial signs to begin using with your baby.

When should I start signing with my baby?

From around 6–7 months is a great age to start using some simple key signs with your baby as this is when children become increasingly receptive to language. Starting earlier than this certainly won't harm your baby, but is usually more beneficial to the parent in allowing signing to be part of their daily life. However, it is important to note that by starting too early some parents may get discouraged and give up if their baby doesn't respond or takes a while to begin signing. At 6–7 months of age, it is actually very easy to encourage and expand a baby's natural communication into the use of sign language on a daily basis. It is usually at home, in context, that your baby will begin to understand and use the basic signs you have shown them, such as for bathtime or bedtime.

> *I think when you start signing, you need to watch them closely to see what things they are interested in, whether it's ducks, buses or, like my son, electricity! Don't worry; there'll be a way to get them started.*
>
> Laura Dodson, mother of Luke

Another, much less scientific, but also valid reason for starting at 6 months+ is because this is the age when your baby is often able, or learning, to sit up unaided (albeit with cushions around them). The benefit of this is threefold: not only does it gives you more freedom to face your baby and sustain excellent eye contact with them, you preserve the freedom to use your hands to sign to them, and in addition, your baby, after accomplishing the epic task of learning to sit up, may well be more able to focus on learning additional skills. Signing will therefore be more manageable for your baby once they are sitting up – it is a great skill to master and so difficult if you are lying on your back, and virtually impossible if you are lying or crawling on your front!

> *I started attending classes when my son was around 6¹/₂ months. Within a couple of weeks he had signed his first sign, 'milk'. We were amazed, and very excited! He would often have his milk after dinner, but I had been busy and forgotten to give it to him. He took it upon himself to remind me. I was amazed that not only could he communicate his needs at such a young age, but it was totally in context and entirely appropriate.*
>
> Jane, mum of Jayden

However, if your baby is already older than 6 or 7 months, don't worry, it's never too late to start signing with your baby. Maybe your baby is not yet talking, or maybe they only have a few words. Perhaps they are now a toddler with an increasing vocabulary. In these cases, do start signing right away, focusing on what they are interested in. You can only enhance your communication with your child, have some fun, and reap the many benefits of signing with your child.

> *Callum started attending signing classes at 16 months old and it has been a most rewarding experience. We both enjoy the classes and use the support material at home.*
>
> *He is now 22 months old and although not yet talking, he communicates his needs perfectly. His first sign was for his bottle of milk and as our extended family uses most of the signs, now everyone knows what he wants.*
>
> *We use Sing and Sign to complete everyday tasks in a fun way, using the 'Change your Nappy' song helps at changing times and the 'Where is it?' sign finds lost toys and clothes!*
>
> *My friends who haven't discovered Sing and Sign are amazed at the signs Callum can make and at the level of communication and understanding we have – without a doubt Sing and Sign has enhanced our lives.*
>
> Vanessa

Guidelines for successful signing

Babies are all unique and you are the ideal judge of what signs will suit your baby best. However, a few simple guidelines will help you along the way. There are plenty of courses and approaches available – Sing and Sign is one of the most popular and has worked for many parents and children, which is the reason why we have used their guidelines and principles. The most important thing to remember is to be consistent with your baby, don't give up, and have fun!

The ten basic guidelines for successful baby signing

Follow these and you can't go wrong!

1 Begin with basics such as *eat, drink, milk, more* and *all gone* (*finished*).
2 Follow your baby's lead.
3 Always say the word as you sign.
4 Speak slowly but naturally.
5 Keep it simple.
6 Happily accept any signing attempts by your baby.
7 Be consistent.
8 Avoid trying to get your baby to 'perform' signs.
9 Be patient and relaxed about baby signing.
10 Praise, praise, praise!

When will my baby start to sign?

Signing comes more quickly for some babies than others, just as speech or walking does. Babies are all gloriously different in the speed and nature of various aspects of their development. From around 6–8 months of age, children become increasingly receptive to language, which is why we recommend showing some key signs from this age. Your baby will start to use the signs you show them when he or she is ready and has something to say. For some, this will be almost as soon as you begin showing them the signs; for others, it may be further down the line. In the meantime, your baby will get a great deal of benefit from simply being signed to in the early stages. This is a sometimes under-estimated stage of the process, which is actually very valuable for your baby. It is important not to be discouraged in any way, but to be consistent in the signs, knowing that you are encouraging communication and strengthening the bond between you and your baby.

> **REMEMBER:** Babies can take just a week or several months before making their first sign, so it is crucial to remember that many benefits of baby signing are achieved long before your baby may use their own signs.

You may hear some amazing and amusing stories of the moment a baby uses their first sign. Some children will be textbook examples of signing 'milk' or 'more' early. Others may begin earlier or later. A few babies (whose parents have been consistent with signing) have been known to sign very little, but have, however, begun to speak earlier than most, with their first words being those that have been signed to them. A baby's initial attempts at signing may not be what you have shown them. For example, quite often the 'more' sign may end up with a child patting the back of their hand – this being a rough approximation of what they have been shown, but adjusted due to his/her dexterity level. You will begin to notice how your child interprets different signs and uses them in context – but more on recognizing your baby's first sign just a little later…

For other babies, 'milk', 'more' or 'eat' aren't the first sign used. 'Duck' for some reason seems a popular favourite for many babies, but many will choose an animal sign as their first sign, such as Laila in the following example.

> Laila was a second child, and at 11 months she was on holiday with her family in Portugal. One of the Portuguese neighbours had an unprecedented amount of dogs tethered by ropes outside his house, which frequently erupted into a wild display of barking and howling, day and night. After a few days of hearing this, Laila's first sign to her mum was obviously 'DOG'.

It is important to try not to put any pressure on your baby to sign early. Your aim should be to make the most of communication at this wonderful and charming stage of development and encourage your baby's sense of wonder and enjoyment.

We had been through a whole term of signing classes and Sasha was 11 months. She absolutely adored every lesson and was the noisiest of all the babies, especially when Jessie cat made an appearance! She still wasn't signing though and we were wondering if she ever would. We went away on holiday and as I let the bath out and my husband put her in her pyjamas, I was taking my time and she suddenly signed 'milk'. Of course Daddy was the first to see it after waiting all that time! We were so delighted and since then, there has been no stopping her, she is now 13 months and picks up almost a sign a day!

Angie Duckett

You will find many illustrations of other parents' experiences of signing with their baby throughout this book. This is to highlight, inspire and encourage you that no two babies are the same – everybody's signing story is different. You will find a great diversity amongst parents' accounts and hopefully some will ring true for you and your family.

Jane's second son began signing earlier than his brother (see the quotation box on page 18), although he only ever used just a few signs up until about the age of 14 months. To begin with his mum would often wonder why, as she had thought she was far more natural with him with regard to her speech and signing, and so therefore far more effective. So why on earth would he take longer?

On reflection, one possible reason he used very few signs early on was because, being a second-time mum, Jane was much more aware of his needs, and was very good at anticipating them. Therefore he had very little reason to express his needs to his mother, as she was probably already well on the way to fulfilling them! Her first son signed 'milk' for the first time purely because she had forgotten to give it to him at his usual time.

So don't get disheartened if your child is taking a while to begin signing, it may purely be that you are a superb parent readily anticipating your child's every need. Be patient and consistent, they will eventually have something to 'say' to you.

Remember, even if you baby is not signing you can be sure that in using some key word signs with your speech you are giving your baby a head start in communication. The advantages to your child begin the very first day you sign '*More?*'. This is because in the early stages of baby signing parents are inclined to:

- speak more slowly so their baby can focus on what they are saying
- think about their child's understanding at a one-word level
- focus on their baby's thought processes and interests
- seek eye contact and shared looking
- repeat and repeat key words
- use a sign to draw their baby's attention to the key word of a sentence.

This concentrated language input sparks connections of understanding and recognition in a baby's developing brain at a very early stage. Babies understand more of what is said to them and they enjoy extra parental attention. The joys of a baby's first sign are the parent's reward, but the babies themselves are reaping enormous developmental benefit from day one.

> **REMEMBER:** If you are using a few signs as part of your daily routine your baby will be listening, watching and learning gradually by your example, while taking great strides in understanding and vocabulary.

Many parents are great at communicating with their children – most will naturally chat to them about all sorts of things, as we are aware this is good for their development and speech. However, what some people aren't so aware of is that the constant dialogue, although very pleasing for your child to hear your voice, isn't always the best way for them to learn to speak. It is also important to vary your speech between plenty of dialogue so your child can understand the ebb and flow of language, and simplified sentences to get the message across. In the latter instance you would sign one word per sentence, recognizing that a child of that age is still understanding at a mono-word level. So instead of saying 'Look, there, did you see that bird in the tree, just up there in the tree'. You would say 'Look, a *bird*' (emphasizing the word but also signing *bird*), 'There is a *bird* up there in the tree'. You will find this naturally slows down your speech and enables your child to understand and begin to try to say and sign the word 'bird'.

Signing has been the most rewarding and useful class I have ever done. I have been able to understand my daughter's wants and needs from an early age (about 12 months) and her speech is just incredible! I have silenced all the critics and non-believers in friends and family and can't recommend it highly enough!

Philippa Mitchell, mum to Paige

Babies will be benefiting enormously from this signing input, but it is not as obvious and immediately rewarding for parents as the next stage, when their baby uses a sign themselves.

Recognizing your baby's first signs

The early signs your baby produces may only be rough approximations of the ones you have shown. This is because, as in all levels of their development, children develop at different rates, so their motor skills and dexterity levels may vary from other children of the same age. For example, a baby may use the sign for 'more' by tapping one hand on the back of the other, or even on the forearm. Some even just clap their hands together or attempt some other variation. This is to be expected and completely normal. The accuracy of a baby's hand shapes when signing is not important at all, it is the message that counts.

How should I respond if I think my baby has started signing?

If you think you have seen a sign used in context then praise your baby by repeating the word in question while modelling the sign correctly. You can also use the opportunity to create meaning from your baby's gesture by allowing your baby to witness the cause and effect of their hand shapes, i.e. 'When I clap, Daddy gives me more; if I want more, all I have to do is clap!' Don't be tempted to adapt your version of the sign to match your baby's. You should be consistent and your baby will refine theirs to match your own over time.

Our signing teacher told us that children all vary in how long they take to sign – for Abigail it was 1 week! The teacher said she thought it was a record and naturally I glowed with maternal pride. She had in fact spent that first week making 'conducting' gestures every time she saw her radio but I didn't really take any notice – until the following week at class when she started 'conducting' every time the singing started. It was the teacher who pointed out that she was doing the sign for music! She'd picked up on the sign but I completely hadn't. I was amazed at just how much she understands and is aware of – so often we assume that because babies can't speak it means they can't understand speech, but how wrong can we be.

Jane Warden, mum to Abigail

Using the same sign for different things

When your child first starts signing, some parents find their baby may use one sign for a while, sometimes in context, and at other times to communicate about everything. You may be thrilled your baby has pointed at the duck in the bath and used the correct sign. Hours later they may use the same sign for your dog! You might find this confusing and somewhat perplexing, thinking your baby seems to be signing meaninglessly, but it is a very common phenomenon and follows exactly the same pattern as a baby's first spoken word. For example, many children will use one word (like 'mama') for many things; so, too, will some children begin by using one sign to mean many different ideas. This really is no bad thing. Your baby has just made a tremendous breakthrough in realizing that the gestures you are using do indeed stand for something and they can be used to get something. Think about that again for a moment: your baby has just understood the concept that a word and sign mean something, and if they repeat that back to you, they may well get what they are wanting! Continue showing them other signs, remain consistent with the signs you are showing your baby, and you will soon see that they are beginning to use the proper signs in the appropriate context.

REMEMBER: Language can be confusing to a baby!

Another reason why your baby may be using the same sign for lots of different objects or concepts is because our wonderful language can often be confusing to them. How often do we say 'Do you want that toy?', 'Can you see that train?', 'Do you want that drink?' or 'That's a sheep.'? Do you see the pattern? Often, without realizing it, we are reinforcing the word THAT – our children then interpret the sign and use it for a huge variety of objects.

Top tip

Often the easy way to avoid confusion in the early stages of signing is to repeat back the word you are signing: 'Do you want that CAR, the CAR?' This not only helps reinforce the sign you are using, but is enabling your baby to listen again to the word associated with the sign.

It seems that after mastering a few signs, most babies suddenly realize that signing will get them what they desire, or are curious about, and their ability to retain signs becomes evident. The other aspect you will then soon begin to notice over a fairly short period of time is your baby refining their attempts to get their message across. This all falls into place soon enough and it is then that many parents will often see an 'explosion' of their baby's signing.

We starting signing when Lilli-Rose was 4 months, she used to sit and watch me, and I became a little disheartened that she didn't sign. I only kept up a few signs – 'more', 'all finished', 'please' and 'thank you'. Just after a year she suddenly started doing all of them, in relation to almost everything she wanted to tell me, i.e. 'more' playing, reading, food, drink etc. I wished I had kept up more signs!

Julia

Case study

Catherine's second son was a very early signer. By the time he came along the family had got into the habit of signing with his older brother, so they thought they were almost naturally signing from birth. As he signed early, they were expecting him to continue very quickly picking up the signs, just as his brother had done – after all, they were showing him so many signs. However, over the next 8–9 months he maintained around ten basic signs, which the family found a little disconcerting. Nevertheless they continued on, because they knew from experience of being in baby signing classes that at around a year, many babies, whatever age they start signing, will really take off and have a 'signing explosion'.

Their son reached a year, and still he continued with the same basic signs. Then around 14½ months he really had a 'signing explosion' and all of a sudden he was rapidly using many of the signs which he had been taught over the months! He had obviously been taking in everything that was being shown to him, and now it seemed all of a sudden he had a lot to 'tell' everyone, and wanted to ensure that he was understood. Sometimes he would give his parents a questioning look, as he watched or noticed something new, and his parents began to become aware of what new things he wanted the word and the accompanying sign for. One of the additional benefits the family observed with the boys is they knew what things were; they were able to effectively communicate (sign) different concepts to people, now they just needed to try out the word. It was very soon after that their son began to drop some of the early signs in favour of speaking those very same words that had been signed to him. Catherine and the rest of the family really began to understand the importance of clearly saying the word that was being signed, and as a result noticed it really helped with both their boys' speech development.

You will find that we will expand a little more on the effectiveness of naming objects, and the head start you are giving your baby, in Chapter 07 'Signing with older children'.

Getting started – your first basic signs

By now you may well have read about what baby signing is, how it started, when you should start signing, when your baby will begin to sign back to you, and how you will recognize their first sign – or you may have just jumped to this section and want to know the actual nuts and bolts of signing with your baby. With all parents we would advise using the ten basic guidelines:

Basic guideline No. 1: Begin with basics such as *eat, drink, milk, more* and *all gone (finished)*.

We would recommend using these signs first, as they are signs that you can use many times during the day – they are an undemanding way to initiate signing. Start by trying to use the signs just at mealtimes, as this will be a routine already familiar with you and a very easy place to start (and you can be sure you are following guideline No. 7 by being consistent!).

EAT

Bear in mind you can go and view all of these signs on the CD accompanying the book. However, for ease now, I am going to explain the very first sign.

How to sign it
Bunch your finger tips together and gently tap the corner of your mouth, emphasize saying the word 'eat' with your baby.

figure 1 eat

When to use it

Begin maybe when you have just finished preparing your baby's meal by saying 'Would you like to *eat*?' as you use the sign. Pop your baby into their chair, finish attaching their bib, and say again 'Would you like to *eat*?' – repeat the sign every time you say the word. As you put down their bowl, or offer them the spoon you can sign and say 'Time to *eat* now'. Alternatively, you can just use the word you are most comfortable with: food, lunch time, snack etc. However, at this point and age of development, the generic word 'eat' is more than sufficient for your baby.

> **REMEMBER:** Always say the word as you sign it. Never sign in silence.

MORE

How to sign it

Make a fist with one hand, and then with the other hand flat, cover it over the top of the fist, just like you are pushing a cork into a bottle. Say 'more'.

figure 2 more

When to use it

Maybe when you have given your baby a few mouthfuls of food, stop and say 'Would you like some *more*?'. You can continue on with this, as a game with your baby. Offer them a few more mouthfuls, then keep stopping and ask if they would like some 'more'.

Top tip

'More' is an ideal first sign as babies always want more of something, whether it be food, drink or another song. When you think your baby wants another game of peek-a-boo, food, drink or cuddle, sign and say 'Would you like some *more*?'

Sam began signing when he was 9 months old. He soon started asking for 'more' and trying other signs.

Sam's cousin, Maddy, started signing classes after we had been singing its praises. His Grandma took him to visit Maddy and a lot of effort was put into trying to get Sam to sign something. He decided he was not going to show off his skills.

They fed the ducks, he just ate the bread.

They waved at people, he just smiled.

Everyone gave up and had afternoon tea. As soon as he was given some cheesecake to eat he started to sign 'more' and would not stop! Even when it was all gone he kept asking for 'more' cheesecake!

His aunt and uncle had not seen a baby sign and thought it was great. It made them more determined to carry on with the lessons.

Su Boardman

DRINK

'Drink' and 'milk' are very easy first signs as well as being signs that can be used many times in a day.

How to sign it

Just like miming drinking from a beaker. Shape your hand as if you are holding a beaker, lift it a few times to your mouth, and say the word 'drink'.

figure 3 drink

When to use it

If you are signing with a young baby of around 6–16 months, we would recommend using the 'drink' sign whether it be for water or juice, or whatever drink you choose to give your baby. Some people like to ask their baby if they are thirsty and then use the drink sign. But it is only when they are slightly older that it can be useful to start giving them choices. We will cover giving your baby choices a little more in Chapter 07, but at this point it is important to consider we are aiming for simplicity, as this is the key to beginning successful signing with your baby.

MILK

'Milk' can be the same sign used for breast or bottle feeding.

All the way through this book you will find we try and give you easy ways of remember the signs you are learning.

> **Top tip**
>
> The easiest way to remember the sign for 'milk' is by thinking of milking a cow!

How to sign it

Make a fist, then open and close your fist as if you are milking, saying the word 'milk'.

figure 4 milk

For those mums who are dual feeding, i.e. using breast and bottle milk, and want a way to differentiate between bottle and breast feeding, an alternative suggestion for milk is for mum to tap both hands just above their chest for 'mummy milk'.

My first daughter Neve joined a signing class in London when she was 6 months old in 2004. It was a brand new class, and baby signing felt very cutting edge at the time. Needless to say, my friends and family were impressed at the concept, but I could tell they were waiting for 'results' before getting enthusiastic. They did not have to wait long.

After only one term, Neve visited her grandparents in Portugal for a spot of sunshine. She became very poorly with the local tummy-bug and I was at my wit's end. She was lying listlessly on her grandma's lap, exhausted and dehydrated, and as I came into the room, she looked at me with desperation in her eyes and did a strong clear 'milk' sign! We were thrilled! We gave her a drink, and she soon perked up.

Vanessa Kreimeia, mother to Neve and Laila

It is probably important to reiterate that although these are the first basic signs to start using with your child, they may not be the first signs they show you. Babies will start signing what they are interested in, or sign something they want to tell you. These signs are great to get you used to signing many times a day with your baby, but don't only show your baby these signs and wait for them to sign back to you before progressing with more signs. If you are in a good routine with your baby, and they are used to food, milk and naps at specific times, then you might find you are so perfectly meeting their needs that they have no need to ask you for milk or a drink at this stage. So don't give up if your baby isn't signing back these basic signs to you. Keep showing them more signs, watching what your baby is interested in – maybe it's animals, or anything with wheels...

Laura found her son's first sign was 'light'. This would be a more unusual sign for a baby to begin with, but beautifully illustrates the point of showing your baby many different signs and focusing on what they are interested in. Laura had been signing all the first basic signs with her son Luke, such as 'eat', 'drink' etc for several weeks but with no response from Luke. Then she noticed that he always looked up at lights in a room – so watching his cues, she started signing it to him. Within a few days Luke had cottoned on. Laura said it was fantastic to be able to communicate and understand what his little mind was interested in.

During the course of this book you will find many different signs to show your baby, and plenty more on the accompanying CD to help provide you with signs that will inspire and engage your baby. Watch what they are interested in, or pointing at, and aim to give them the appropriate sign.

ALL GONE/FINISHED

How to sign it

Begin by holding your fists together with your palms facing inwards, then move your hands out so your hands are flat and facing down, saying 'all gone'.

figure 5 all gone/finished

When to use it

'All gone' or 'finished' is a versatile sign to use many times throughout the day, not only at mealtimes. When you have finished feeding, your peek-a-boo game is over, the story book you were reading to your baby has finished, when a TV programme has ended, or a visitor leaves the house, try using the 'all gone' (finished) sign.

When you have to disappoint your baby because something is over, this sign is unequivocal. Using the 'all gone' sign consistently will help your baby overcome the many little disappointments they face. You may not believe it until you try it, but it does! 'All gone' is often one of the first signs to be initiated by babies.

> **REMEMBER:** The more you use a certain sign, the more likely it is that your baby will start to recognize it in context and anticipate what is about to happen. Get in the habit of using these signs and aim to adopt them as a natural and habitual part of daily routines. Repetition and consistency is the key to successful baby signing.

Basic guideline No. 2: Follow your baby's lead

We have hinted at this already, but from 9 months onwards, watch carefully to see what interests your baby and follow their lead. Begin to introduce signs for those words your baby might want to say, or is beginning to point at.

Each baby has different interests and while one enthusiastically points to and gets excited by anything to do with wheels, another may be fascinated by the family cat or the swings in the park. You know your child, and you know what other signs will be the most motivating for them. As your baby points to something of interest, then looks back to you, start showing them the relevant signs. Babies and children generally have an insatiable appetite to learn more about the world around them; therefore they will require more signs to satisfy their ever-increasing needs, desires and curiosities.

Basic guideline No. 3: Always say the word as you sign

This is especially significant, and an area where Sing and Sign differs from some American and English programmes which would advocate maintaining some form of silent communication. Clearly, your child will not want to hear your lovely voice from morning until night, and there will be times where you may sit quietly having a cuddle, or just sit quietly gathering your thoughts (if that is at all possible with a young baby). However, when you are communicating with your baby, and using a sign, you must *always say the word*.

> **REMEMBER:** Our aim when using a sign is to encourage and develop our children's speech, which cannot be achieved when using the sign alone. Therefore it cannot be overstated how important it is to ALWAYS say the word as you sign it.

By doing this, you are giving your child verbal and visual encouragement to communicate with you. Your child will pick up the visual clue, but also clearly hear the word behind the sign. This is why the words that you sign are often your baby's first spoken words.

Basic guideline No. 4: Speak slowly, but naturally

Try and speak a little slower than usual but in a natural way, maintaining eye contact if possible. As you adjust your speech slightly, you will give your child a greater chance to pick up on and process exactly what you are saying. Many parents can be great at providing their child with rich language in large quantities, speaking at a regular speed. This is a vital part of exposing your child to variety in language. However, when you begin to sign with your child, it is recommended you should sign just the one word in a sentence. You will find this will slow your speech down, and enable your child to begin speaking the words you are signing. Quite often this will be earlier than their (non-signing) peers.

> **REMEMBER:** Don't slow your speech down to the point it becomes stilted, but certainly slow it down enough to speak the specific word you are signing and to repeat it if necessary.

Eye contact and facial expressions provide important social and emotional information; people, perhaps without consciously doing so, probe each other's eyes and faces for positive or negative mood signs. Eye contact shows personal involvement and creates intimate bonds. Recent studies also suggest that eye contact has a positive impact on the retention and recall of information and may promote more efficient learning. Some parents will not realize the full benefit of maintaining good eye contact with a young baby. One parent remarked that it wasn't until they had an active toddler on their hands, who wanted to be, and do, everything, that they suddenly began realizing the wisdom of what they had been teaching their baby. When the baby became a much stronger-willed toddler, their earlier training meant it was so much more natural for them to have hold of him, on his level, maintaining good eye contact with him, whilst giving him instruction, or indeed just telling him how much they loved him! The message that you are imparting always penetrates that much deeper when maintaining good eye contact.

Basic guideline No. 5: Keep it simple

Use just one sign per sentence when speaking with your baby. The more signs you learn, the more tempted you may be to use more than you need. Nevertheless, the magic of baby signing actually lies in its simplicity. Although you can use as many interesting signs as you like with your baby, just remember to use *only one sign per sentence*. For example, you may see a cat in your garden and want to draw your baby's attention to it. You would continue to speak normally, saying and signing 'Look, do you see that little *cat*. Look, it's just about to climb the big fir tree. Can you see the little *cat*?' The main focus for your baby's attention is the cat, so although you may know the signs for 'little', 'big' and 'tree' and have effectively used them on many other occasions, it is important to keep in mind you must maintain using the simple key word approach with your baby at this stage of development.

> **REMEMBER:** Just use one sign per sentence. You may get to the point in your child's development when they begin signing more than one word per sentence, showing off their skills, but maintain your stance of using one sign per sentence.

The exception to this rule is when signing along to action songs, as you will often use more than one sign in each phrase of the song and will therefore have the opportunity to practise your fluency and co-ordination. So while you learn signs from songs, your baby will learn gradually and naturally from your everyday exchanges, and the signs you use in context at home.

Basic guideline No. 6: Happily accept any signing attempts by your baby

Even approximate imitations of the signs you show should be accepted. As we have already discussed in 'Recognizing your baby's first signs' on page 23, you may not get an exact representation of the sign you are showing your baby. A perfect sign is not what we are aiming to achieve, increased communication between you and your baby is a far better ideal to aim for. As long as you are recognizing the sign your baby is giving you, and the meaning your baby attaches to that sign, then show your baby lots of enthusiasm and praise for attempting to sign – although from experience this will come incredibly naturally to most parents who cannot contain their excitement at their baby's first sign!

Basic guideline No. 7: Be consistent

Be consistent in how you show a sign, however your baby adapts it. If you are consistent in using the signs you have chosen, your baby will be noticing, listening and learning gradually by your example while taking great strides in comprehension and vocabulary. You may think that if your baby uses the 'more' sign, for instance, by tapping their forearm (instead of the hand coming down to cover the fist) that you should copy their interpretation of the sign. However, this will greatly confuse your baby who is used to seeing you use the sign correctly. In general, the more your baby sees you sign, or sees a particular sign, the quicker they will recognize it, the quicker they learn it and therefore start using it for themselves.

Basic guidleine No. 8: Avoid trying to get your baby to 'perform' signs for relatives or friends

As excited as you may be when your child has begun signing, avoid the temptation of making them perform. Signing should remain fun for you and your child, and an easy way to communicate. It should not have the added pressure of pleasing an audience, however appreciative that audience may be. The more natural you are when signing with your child and the more your child has to say, the more they will naturally sign. Family and friends will not be able to fail to notice your baby signing once they start.

Basic guideline No. 9: Be patient and relaxed about baby signing

Enjoy the process of communicating with your child, regardless of their signing attempts. Signing can become a very natural part of your communication with your child so try and maintain a relaxed approach with them. Think about the most popular sign or gesture parents often use with their child – waving hello or goodbye. This is often done enthusiastically, signing and saying the word, without any embarrassment of what others might think of them. This is how all signing should be with your child

– easy, effortless and natural. Again, begin with the basics and gradually build up your signs, signing whenever possible.

Remember, signing with your baby should be fun, giving you time to focus on things your baby may enjoy or be interested in.

Basic guideline No. 10: Praise, praise, praise!

We all know how well people, and especially children, respond to praise and encouragement. If you think you have seen a sign used in context then praise your baby, however fragile the attempt. You can also take this opportunity to repeat the word and the sign back to your baby, ensuring, of course, that you are consistent with your sign, and modelling it correctly. If your baby's attempts at signing are rewarded with the response they wanted, they will be far more motivated to learn more signs, therefore enhancing your communication with your baby even further.

03

the next steps

In this chapter you will learn:
- how to use signs within your established routines
- signs which may be motivating for your child
- simple songs to use when preparing to go out or change your child's nappy
- ideas for implementing signs at home.

Introducing signs relevant to your child's world

At this point, you are hopefully mastering the first basic signs of 'eat', 'drink', 'milk', 'more' and 'all gone' – and beginning to use those signs many times during the day. Keep in mind that mealtimes are a great time to use all of the first basic signs. Maybe your baby has begun to recognize them and respond when you use them, or maybe your baby is already starting to use them. Whatever stage you are at, keep persevering with signing – remember, you may not be able to see the benefits at this stage, but you will be expanding your baby's language and comprehension.

The next five signs will also fit the same category and be signs that will be used frequently during the day. There is no harm in using as many signs as you can remember. Using these signs as descriptive gestures to support some of these important words will help your baby understand and remember what they mean.

Early basics: *where, help, open, yes, no*

WHERE

When to use it

A fun way to introduce other family members to your baby's signing is through playing simple hiding games with cuddly toys. Grandparents especially love to play and interact with their grandchildren. Begin by showing them a simple game using the 'where' sign.

Most babies love to play 'peek-a-boo' and in fact any game that involves finding a favourite toy. 'Where' is one of those gestures that many parents will naturally use with their baby.

How to sign it

Hold your hands in front of you with palms facing upwards, making small circles, saying 'where'.

figure 6 where

> *The most fun sign with Jacob is 'where'. He loves to hide things (or himself) and sign 'where' before popping back out with a 'boo'!*
>
> Chris with Jacob aged 1

If your baby is enjoying playing a hiding game with you then use the 'where' sign when the cuddly toy has been hidden, and of course the 'more' sign if your baby is enjoying the game. When it's time to stop, you can also make use of the 'all gone' or 'finished' sign.

> *Ben adopted the 'where' sign very quickly after he starting signing (aged 13 months) and has used it, enthusiastically, to play hide and seek games with his parents and other relatives ever since. He has been able to take the lead in hiding an object and telling his family to do the seeking (using the 'where' sign), enabling him to communicate proactively, developing his confidence and displaying a cheeky sense of humour in a way that, without signing, would have been impossible at such a young age.*
>
> Jane Kirkby and Ben

HELP

Many babies like the 'help' sign and it is a sign that can significantly reduce frustration, especially with a child desperate to achieve something, but who is unable to do so without some added input.

How to sign it

With outstretched arms, make the thumbs up sign with your right hand, put this hand on top of your upturned left palm, then move both hands together towards your chest, saying 'Help'.

figure 7 help

When to use it

You can say 'Shall I *help* you with ...?', clearly demonstrating the help sign. It won't be long before your baby will be using the sign to ask for your help.

Case study

Michelle was interacting with her young daughter when Melissa began frantically signing 'help' to her mum. Michelle, quickly recognizing her daughter's sign and increasing frustration, went over to her and said and signed:

'What? Melissa, what do you want help with?'

Melissa then quickly signed 'rabbit' followed by 'where'. Her mum again quickly responded with 'Oh, you want to know where your rabbit is? I tidied up and put it in the toy box.' With that it was taken out of the toy box and returned to a very happy Melissa, who then sat cuddling her favourite rabbit.

Note how this short interaction between Melissa and her mum enabled Melissa to simply yet effectively communicate her needs to her mother, and how straightforward it was for her mother to decipher her daughter's desires. There are many other non-signing babies who will have similar wants in finding a favourite cuddly toy, or other prized possession, but the outcome would have been very different – possibly resulting in escalating frustration when mum didn't understand baby's pointing, grunting and possibly crying and, for some no doubt, a full blown temper tantrum would have ensued. This is a true life example of how signing can help and aid simple communication with your baby.

OPEN

'Open' is another particularly useful sign to use with your baby, and so easy too.

How to sign it
Just scrunch your hand up, and with a big flourish, open your fingers out, saying 'open'.

When to use it
This sign is particularly good for facial expressiveness and should be said with a nice, high, light voice. As well as being easy for babies' hands to master, 'open' is a sign that really motivates because the resulting reward is instant, especially if you are about to give your baby a treat. Whenever you open something that your baby is about to enjoy, such as a yoghurt or a toy box, use the sign to show them what you are doing.

Quick game: If you want to play a great game with your baby, incorporating the 'open', 'where', and 'all gone' signs, why not use a simple pillowcase or bag to hide a few favourite toys? Ask your baby 'Where is ...?' Surprisingly quickly, babies enter into the game and point to the pillowcase/bag. This is the ideal time to use the 'open' sign, and produce the toy with a great flourish. This hiding game can go on all the while your baby maintains interest. Don't forget to use the 'all gone' sign at the end of the game.

NO

This 'no' sign is wonderful as it illustrates perfectly the expressiveness of a simple gesture, and a very clear message is present in the body language.

How to sign it

Use a flat hand facing away from your body, and make one movement starting in front of your body, taking your hand out to the side, saying 'no' clearly.

figure 8 no

When to use it

Use this sign any time you are using such language as 'no', 'don't touch', 'mustn't' etc.

You can also leave the sign in the air, while the message of what you are saying sinks in. By recommending you use a clear and consistent 'no' sign, we are not in any way encouraging you to be negative with your baby. Generally, it is always better to put something in a positive rather than a negative way with your child. However, there are times when a 'don't touch', for instance, is appropriate if a child is about to touch something hot.

> As Chloe has become more mobile, I have had to use the sign and say the word 'no' more often. Chloe clearly understands the sign and tone of voice I use. Often, all I have to do is say her name and say 'no', she will look at me and repeat the sign before moving onto something else.
>
> Jeanette Luck

Some people might find that their baby is very adaptable to signing – for example, while many babies' first word might be 'no', the signing child might quickly learn this sign as an alternative form of protest.

> **Top tip**
> If your baby frequently likes to head towards the fireplace, or any other items in your house that are impossible to move, and therefore out of bounds for them, try calling their name when they head towards it and clearly say 'Don't touch', adding the 'no' sign. Try leaving your hand in the air for a few moments in order for the visual cue to continue after you have said the words – this will leave your baby in no doubt about what you are saying.

> *Finn was 11 months old and walking confidently. Typically, he was into absolutely everything including a freestanding bedside lamp. The 'no' sign is obviously a well used sign and my baby in his attempt to grab the lamp and pull it over, was told 'no' using the sign. To my amazement he signed it back to me, with a great big grin on his face. Not only was he now signing, he was using it with humour! Finn's signing has now taken off and all members of the family use it readily and with confidence.*
>
> Julie Neville with Finn

The 'no' gesture covers a wide range of words and can help your baby's growing understanding of everyday language such as 'don't', 'mustn't', 'didn't', 'none', 'never', 'nothing', 'no more'... this list could go on and on, but the sign is the same and is very simple. Again this is another example of using a generic sign to cover many words, and the essential principal of keeping signing simple with your baby.

> **REMEMBER:** Even when your baby is older and able to talk and say the word 'no', this remains one of those very useful signs that is worth continuing to sign with your child.

Parents have often commentated on how useful they found using the 'no' sign, especially at busy parent and child type activities when their lively toddler was across the other side of a room. Without seeming to be parents who shout at their children, they could shout their child's name to gain their attention, and then sign 'no' whilst trying to reach them. It would often stop them in their tracks long enough to avoid a difficult or dangerous situation. Eventually, you may be able to use the sign without needing to move from your chair. If you get into the habit of using the 'no' sign you will find the sign does the shouting for you.

Case study

Maya is 11 months old and we have been going to baby signing for a few weeks.

I was looking forward to teaching her the signs but the only one she has got is 'no'. And I know the exact moment she learnt it. I was trying to stop her climbing on the cabinet to the TV and she had previously responded to a verbal 'no' after I had taken her away several times. After a while, she pushed the boundaries and grinned at me as she edged to the telly.

I let her go so far and then said 'no' and signed it clearly, looking her in the eye. She started to cry a little and I told her why she couldn't. And again put my hand up. Instead of crying she sat and stared at me for a clear minute. I ignored her. For about a month after she was grouchy with me and became a daddy's girl and I worried that I had gone too far and maybe broken our bond.

Today we were playing really happily and she had had enough of dinner, she had been closing her mouth but I wasn't sure if she was just messing or hadn't finished the last mouthful. She obviously got fed up. Looking totally exasperated, she signed 'no' and shook her head. I laughed and told her it was OK if she had finished.

She looked so happy to be finally understood, and to have a voice of her own that mummy also respected. I think our bond is stronger than ever.

Tara Mills

YES

'Yes' is possibly not a sign that your young baby will use early on, but goes hand-in-hand with the 'no' sign, so this is therefore a useful place in the book to show you this sign.

How to sign it

Make a fist with your right hand and 'nod' yes (from your wrist) with your hand, saying 'Yes', at the same time.

figure 9 yes

When to use it

'Yes' is a sign that is often used when giving your baby choices – 'Would you like a breadstick – *yes*?' You will find you can use it many times with lift the flap books – 'Who is under rug? Is it the dog? *Yes* – there he is!' Older babies and toddlers love to use this sign when asked a question, however, the earlier you expose your baby to these signs and establish a meaning with them, the earlier they will understand and begin to take advantage of using the sign, which for some babies you may find interlinked with their verbal communication.

With younger babies, begin by emphasizing the word 'yes' at a time when you are confident this is their likely answer to a question, i.e. 'Would you like an apple/chocolate biscuit?' If their eyes light up at the thought of food, introduce the sign within your sentence, – i.e. '*Yes* – you would like an apple'.

It shouldn't be too long before your baby is trying the sign or to say the word themselves. Bear in mind, however, that this is very age dependant; younger children's 'yes' may simply come out as a 'sssssss'. Once your child has grasped the concept of what 'yes' means, you might like to try moving onto what we would call at this age a 'parent-pleasing sign' which is 'please'.

For example: Your child has appropriately responded to the question 'Would you like an apple?' by either signing, or saying 'yes'. This is therefore a fitting time to introduce the word and sign 'please' (you can see this sign in Chapter 04, 'Love and manners'). This continues to keep your signing at a one-word focus level, which is age appropriate, but moving your baby on to introduce further concepts and ideas. In doing this, some babies will revert to just signing the word 'please' if they want something. However, it is important to note, at this point of development manners are far more important to parents than babies, which is why signs such as 'please' and 'thank you' are referred to as parent-pleasers. This is in no way negating the importance of manners, but to recognize that the relevance for a 6-month-old won't be the same as for an 18-month-old with a wider vocabulary and understanding. Babies will sign what they are interested in, so signs which incorporate manners tend to come much further down the list and are generally used with older babies.

Routines: going out, nappy changing, bath and bed

We all know how much babies love and thrive on routines. In this next section, we will be using straightforward concepts and simple themes that will begin to extend your baby's growing understanding. All the concepts and themes are based on the vocabulary of your baby's world. By providing additional signs to everyday events, you will be increasing your signing repertoire, as well as providing your baby with concrete illustrations of events that are about to happen. This in turn will aid their comprehension and eventually their vocabulary.

LET'S GO OUT

A baby's world is really quite small, so going out is a major event and something babies will usually get excited about. Too often we can make a decision to go to the shops, visit a friend, walk the dog, and so on, and we start packing the nappy bag, get our shoes, coat and even our baby's shoes on without our baby even knowing what is going on – we have failed to communicate with them what we are doing, and where we are going. Below are some of the basic signs which are perfect at this age to incorporate into your going out routine, ensuring your baby is calm and confident in knowing what is coming next.

GOING OUT

How to sign it
Cup your hand slightly, palm facing downwards, and mime 'going over the wall' – remembering to say 'we are going out'.

figure 10 going out

When to use it
Use 'going out' to signal the beginning of preparations for departure. We recommend showing signs for the places you visit regularly – maybe it's the park, shops or swimming pool. (It might be worth noting at this point that all of these signs can be seen on the accompanying CD. However, some signs are so simple and do not need pictures that I will just provide a brief explanation.)

SHOPS

How to sign it
With two hands starting close to your chest, mime pushing a trolley, so as you extend, 'push' your arms in front.

SWIMMING POOL

How to sign it
Mime doing breast stroke.

FARM

How to sign it

Think of a farmer wearing braces. With both thumbs mime pulling braces forward.

MUSIC (CLASS)

How to sign it

With index fingers in the air, wave from side to side as if conducting.

PARK

How to sign it

With a flat hand facing downwards, make a wide circle from your waist.

When at the park, what does your baby enjoy doing? Maybe they love being pushed on the swings, going fast down the slide, or perhaps you have a sandpit they love to play in? As these are activities babies generally enjoy, they are highly motivating signs and therefore ones that many babies will use. Try to use these when at the park, or even in your own back garden.

SWINGS

How to sign it

Two hands mime a swing action by your sides. Remember to say 'swings'.

figure 11 swings

SLIDE

How to sign it
Flat hand mimes sliding down.

SAND

How to sign it
Think of rubbing flour through your fingers, do this action whilst raising your hands upwards, saying 'sand'.

figure 12 sand

♪

> We're going to the *park*
> We're going to the *park*,
> Ee-i-a-dio we're going to the *park*

♪

It's been fantastic to be able to know what our baby is thinking when we are walking down the street. He'll often stop to 'tell' us about some birds or flowers he has seen. Signing has brought a great richness to our relationship with Jacob and we feel very privileged to know him so well.

Chris Miles with Jacob aged 12 months

As much as babies love to go out, sometimes it can be difficult getting them there. Communicating where you are going and what you are doing may generally make things easier, but sometimes not even that will help. The first thing you may begin a battle with is putting on their shoes or maybe their coat...

COAT

How to sign it
Mime pulling a coat around your shoulders

SHOES

How to sign it
With one hand make a 'bridge' and mime putting a 'shoe' on the other hand. Remember to say 'shoe'.

figure 13 shoes

When to use it
Don't forget to use this sign as you are putting your baby's shoes on. You can then let them know if you are going for a walk – so you can use the sign for 'buggy' or 'going out' – or maybe this is a journey you are making on public transport or in the car. All are simple signs which you can incorporate into your signing repertoire.

BUGGY

How to sign it
Mime pushing a buggy in front of you.

BUS

How to sign it
With arms parallel to your shoulders and straight arms, mime a big steering wheel.

CAR

How to sign it
With hands in front of you and bent arms, mime a small steering wheel.

Wherever you are going, whatever you are doing, and however you are getting there, try to let your baby know as much as possible, using a few of these easy signs.

On getting ready to go out, you may find your conversation goes something like this:

'Come on then, we are *going out*'. Your child may look up at you, so you can respond to their look by replying, 'Yes, we are *going out*'. Pick up your child, or take them to where you can then begin to put their shoes on. Sitting them back down again, you can say 'Come on, let's put your *shoes* on.' This would be a great time to try out the song on page 54 to help you make this, sometimes difficult time in getting a child ready into a fun way of preparing to go out the door. Finally, with shoes, coat, bag and child all set, you can let them know you are going in the *buggy*, *bus* or the *car*. Once safely strapped in the buggy or the car (but before you drive off), it would be a good time to try and tell your child where you are going – the *park*, *shops*, the *swimming pool*, or maybe a *music class*. By using an appropriate sign, it won't be long before your child will have an understanding of all the places you regularly visit and your baby can predict what comes next.

You may be surprised one day, when you tell your toddler you are going out, that they simply sign shoes to you, or they toddle off to get their own shoes. Many parents have testified to that type of scenario with their own children, and have come to fully understand the value and power of using signs in context during everyday situations.

The value in signing to get over these sometimes difficult moments cannot be overstated. It somehow seems that doing things rhythmically gets children moving in a way that persuasion and even bribery cannot. You may be aware of the traditional nursery rhyme 'Here we go round the mulberry bush'. This can be sung as 'Here we go and put on our shoes' or 'Here we go…' doing practically anything! This song is great for fitting most things. It can be really beneficial with preparing to go out, making it so much easier and a lot more fun – why not try it yourself?

♪

'This is the way we put on our *shoes*
Put on our *shoes*
Put on our *shoes*
This is the way we put on our *shoes*
On a cold and frosty morning'

♪

'This is the way we put on our *hat*
Put on our *hat*
Put on our *hat*
This is the way we put on our *hat*
On a warm and sunny day-ay'

♪

HAT

How to sign it
With a flat hand, put a 'hat' on your head, by patting your head.

When to use it
Great to use when you are going out on a hot summer's day or indeed when you are wrapping up warm and snug in winter months.

Your child may love going out, or walking down the road to the shops. However, for some it can become a huge trial. You may be a parent who has difficulty getting down the road because your toddler has other ideas. Playing simple games and using simple melodies such as 'walk and stop', 'march and stop' etc. can help you to complete an otherwise simple journey without too much difficulty. You can be inventive and make up your own words and tunes. Your baby will absolutely love your singing attempts, even if others would cover their ears!

HOME

'Home' is a particularly important sign: it represents a refuge and safe haven for your baby. Wherever you are, inevitably it will eventually be time to go 'home'.

How to sign it

Mime a roof, saying 'home' as your fingertips touch.

figure 14 home

This is a very simple sign, but eloquently provides your baby with a very clear illustration of what is about to happen. Just as your going out routine provides your baby with the stability of being able to predict what comes next, don't forget to let them know when it is time to go home. For some babies, this sign is a welcome relief, and for others it can cause upset if they have to leave a favourite activity they have been enjoying. For Jess in the following example, it was a sign she used, but wasn't understood.

> *My daughter was collected from nursery by her Nana and*
> *Grandad a few weeks ago. When they arrived she was sat with*
> *one of the workers whilst she waited, repeatedly doing a sign.*
> *They said they wished they knew what she had been trying to say,*
> *and showed me the sign... she had been signing 'Home'.*
>
> Jo Mitchell and Jess

The above example not only illustrates how much your baby can understand and communicate their wishes, it also shows the importance of letting significant people in your baby's world know the signs your baby is using, so they can more appropriately respond to their needs. We will cover important people in your baby's world, and signing within a nursery setting, in a little more detail in Chapter 05.

♪

'We're going to the *park*
We're going to the *park*,
Ee-i-a-dio we're going to the *park*
And now we're going *home*
Now we're going *home*
Ee-i-a-dio, now we're going *home*.'

♪

Nappy time

Another occurrence which takes place with alarming regularity in your baby's world is being required to change endless nappies in the course of a day.

CHANGE (NAPPY)

How to sign it

Hold your fists together and twist from side to side saying 'change your nappy'.

figure 15 change nappy

Some babies lie perfectly still – many wriggle and squirm. Obviously trying to sign and change a nappy at the same time is just not going to work, so in this instance you could try the trusted routine of singing to your baby whilst changing: nappy time, bathtime, why not use it as 'sing along time'. Even if you think your singing is not up to scratch, your baby will *love* to hear it. It is amazing that a simple solution, such as singing, can ease problem areas when relating to your child.

> **Top tip**
> Try to use as many fun songs as you can for some very important daily routines.

This wonderfully simple nappy song can be sung to the tune of *Frere Jacques*.

♪

'*Change* your nappy, *change* your nappy,
Carefully, carefully
Throw it in the dustbin, throw it in the dustbin,
Now you're *clean*, nice and *clean*!'

♪

If you use cloth or washable nappies you could sing 'Throw it in the wash bin', 'Throw it in the bucket' or even 'Chuck it in the bucket!' if you prefer!

> *I am most grateful to Sing and Sign for one thing that has made our lives 1000 times easier. As soon as she could crawl, Abigail flatly refused to lie still to have her nappy changed. This was becoming a frustrating nightmare for all of us until her first week of signing classes – she learnt the sign for 'monkey' and was able to tell me that if I sang the right song (the one about the monkeys) she was happy to lie still. So, I gauge how many monkeys need to be bouncing on the bed according to how long I think it will take to change her nappy and she lies there very happily doing every single sign for that song and letting me change her nappy with no fuss at all. It really feels like a miracle!*
>
> Jane Warden

DIRTY and CLEAN

How to sign it

DIRTY– *Rub the inside of your wrists together, just as if you have dirty cuffs. Remember to say the word 'dirty' as you do it.*

figure 16 dirty

CLEAN – *Have one upturned palm, and then sweep your other open palm across it, saying 'clean'.*

figure 17 clean

When to use it

'Dirty' and 'clean' are signs that are easy to use with the routines of changing nappies and bathtime. However, they can be great to use with any messy activity you may participate in with your child, from painting and play dough to getting muddy in the garden. For some parents, using the 'dirty' and 'clean' signs in particular can be the prelude to successfully potty training their children. Parents can begin with initially using the 'dirty' sign at the very first indication of a soiled nappy, and then on a completion of a nappy change, using the 'clean' sign. For some fortunate parents, their child picks up on these signs, and it isn't too long before their child is able to communicate to them when they have a dirty nappy. Eventually, most of these children will use the 'dirty' sign as a pre-cursor to a soiled nappy – letting their parents know they need the potty. However, it is important to note, signing isn't an automatic pre-cursor to earlier potty training; it is just another way for your baby to communicate his or her needs to you. As with all that has been recommended so far, use as many signs as you can with your baby (only one per sentence though) and they will choose which ones are of most benefit to them.

> **Top tip**
> Use as many signs as possible for the various activities and routines you have throughout the day. This gives your baby the opportunity to choose which signs benefit them the most, and therefore enhance communication with you.

Bath and bed

As with meal times, your baby's nightly bedtime routine is a great point in the day in which to introduce some further signs to aid and encourage your child's vocabulary. Ideally, you are trying to create a calm, quiet, relaxed atmosphere where you and your baby have intimate moments, whispered words and lots of hugs and kisses. Depending on your child, that may well be the reality for you on a daily basis, but if you are on baby number two, three or even four, that may well not be the case. However, the things you do that occur every night will form part of your bedtime ritual with your baby, and easily allow you to familiarize yourself with some extra signs, in context, night after night. This will give your baby the clear signal that it is time to make the transition from day to night, from activity to sleep, and therefore isn't dependant on what else may be happening in the household. Nowadays most parents are told it is unnecessary to bath their baby every single night, so that may not be part of your daily routine, but it is still a great occasion for your baby, and one that is normally met with squeals of delight.

BATH

How to sign it

Cross your arms over your chest and mime washing yourself. Remember to say 'bath'.

figure 18 bath

When to use it

You can start by saying 'It's time for your *bath* (doing the sign), lets go to the bathroom'. Undoubtedly, you will be removing your baby's nappy, so don't forget to try and use the 'nappy change' sign, and maybe sing the nappy song (see page 57).

Again just before putting your baby in the bath, you can reiterate what you are doing, saying 'You're going in the *bath* now'. Keep discussing and using the 'bath' sign as much as possible during your bathtime routine, as repetition is a key to learning for babies and children.

Most babies will love going in the bath for a splash, and this can be a great time to use many further signs with your baby, especially if you happen to fill your bath with plenty of toys. The signs for duck, boat and fish are always popular early signs for babies (these can be found in the next section, see page 65) so don't forget to keep using all these signs – even during bathtime.

> **REMEMBER:** Repetition is the key to learning for young babies and children, so try to use as many of these signs on a daily basis as you can.

Bedtime routines are so important; the consistency you have will help your child be fully aware of what is happening next and therefore they will feel more secure during bedtime. This can be especially important if you have a sensitive child who needs help adjusting in learning the transition from being together to being apart from you.

Now you have a nice *clean* baby all tucked up and ready for bed. Does your baby go *upstairs* for bed? Maybe you give some *milk* as a last feed? Or maybe it's straight onto *brushing* their *teeth*/gums. Use as many signs as you can remember, and try each day to build more signs in during the bedtime rituals.

UPSTAIRS

How to sign it

Let your first and middle fingers of one hand make a walking movement 'up' invisible stairs.

BRUSHING TEETH

How to sign it

Very simply, with your index finger, mime brushing your front teeth.

You will find that brushing teeth is generally something babies love or hate, although for some this experience is normally just an excuse to bite the toothbrush! Why not try a simple rhyme to the tune of 'Here we go round the mulberry bush'?

♪

> This is the way we **brush our teeth**
> **Brush our teeth**
> **Brush our teeth**
> This is the way we **brush our teeth**
> Before we go to bed – ed.

♪

TIRED

How to sign it

Clench your fist and rub your eye.

When to use it

Once bathtime, nappy change and teeth cleaning have been accomplished, this might be the perfect opportunity to tell your baby they are *tired*. This can easily be followed by a loud yawn using your hand to pat your mouth. Even if your baby is not tired at this point, you may well be, but still try to make your signing as expressive as possible with different sounds and facial expressions, as your baby will respond positively to these.

So do you quietly sit in a rocking chair for a few minutes, or simply pop your baby into their cot? Maybe you read them a story first? You could ask them if they would like a *book*?

BOOK

How to sign it

With both hands clasped together mime opening a book

Many children's books will give you ample opportunity to use countless different signs you have learnt.

At this point in your nightly routine, there is no doubt that your baby knows it's time for 'bed'.

BED

How to sign it

Put your hands together on one side of your face, and then tilt your head – just as if your hands are becoming your pillow.

As you tuck them in, do they have something to help them settle? Maybe it's a special *teddy*, a favourite *doll* or some other comforter?

TEDDY

How to sign it

Gently clawed hands cross, and hands tap your shoulders – almost as if you are making a cuddle gesture. Say 'teddy'.

figure 19 teddy

DOLL

How to sign it

Hands in rocking position, but held still, saying 'doll'.

figure 20 doll

MUSLIN

How to sign it

Make a fist, facing inwards, rub this up and down on your cheek. Remember to say 'muslin'.

figure 21 muslin

When to use it

This sign can be used not only for a muslin, but for any other comforter your child may use.

When you begin to use these signs and label your baby's world in this way, describing with words, noise, signs and facial expressions the different routines you have, you and your baby can share a lovely conversation at bedtime about what you have done together and where you have been. Don't forget, your baby can comprehend what you are saying, and through signing can communicate their understanding to you long before they are able to talk. You may be amazed at what your baby has to share with you.

Motivating signs: animals and vehicles

Why do we call 'animals and vehicles' 'motivating signs'? You think your baby is unlikely ever to have an urgent need to tell you they have just seen a lion in the high street? Think again. Animal pictures, animal toys and animal references make up a major part of a small baby's world. From the monkey picture on his drinking cup, to the giraffes on her curtains and the dog in his favourite book, your child sees animals everywhere. Even more exciting is that your baby loves to talk about them.

> I started signing with my daughter relatively late, when she was about 13 months, after a friend introduced us to it via the Sing and Sign DVD. She picked up signs very quickly and signed them back. Her first and firm favourites for some time were cat and duck. One of the funniest occasions of her signing 'duck' early on, was when we were house hunting. We were looking at the bathroom of a house and she was signing insistently duck at us. We couldn't see any ducks there – the owners were an older couple and there were no obvious signs of ducks in the bathroom, however she had spotted the light switch had a duck attached to it.
>
> Helen Tillinghast, mum to Eloise and Joshua

Babies will often notice things that we take for granted or simply just fail to notice. They will also sign for those things they hear as well as observe.

Ask any parent of a signing baby what their baby's favourite signs are and animals of all shapes and sizes will feature strongly. So here are a few to be getting on with. You can find many more on the accompanying CD.

ANIMALS

How to sign it
With palms facing down, mime 'prowling' hands going forward.

CAT

How to sign it
With both hands making 'V' shapes with first two fingers, mime whiskers coming from your nose out. Don't forget to say 'cat'.

figure 22 cat

DOG

How to sign it
Index and third fingers of both hands move down once in front of your chest, saying 'dog'.

figure 23 dog

FISH

How to sign it

Your hand faces sideways and mimes a fish tail movement 'swimming'. Remember to say 'fish'.

figure 24 fish

You may think that you are always introducing things to your baby's world, and for a while it may feel like a one-way street. However, by signing you are giving your child a way to express things to you and an opportunity to 'tell' you what is important in their world, long before they can verbalize it.

BIRD

How to sign it

With your thumb and index finger of one hand, open and close several times (keep the other 3 fingers clenched) – just as if you are doing a mime for opening and closing a bird's beak.

BEE

How to sign it

Again with your thumb and index finger together, make random loops in the air. Great with a good bzzzzzzz sound too!

DUCK

How to sign it
A sign you may naturally do with your baby, but just as if your hand is a beak, open and close your whole hand as if your were making a 'quacking' move.

ELEPHANT

How to sign it
Make a fist, take it up to your nose and mime a big trunk, with a little flourish at the end.

CROCODILE

How to sign it
Think of your hands and arms as the jaws of a croc, so with both hands mime a big snapping action.

CHICKEN

How to sign it
Your elbows become wings, so move them in and out, just like a chicken.

MONKEY

How to sign it
For this one, there is nothing for it but to look like a monkey, so with both arms stretched out horizontally, bend them at the elbow and start scratching under your arms!

RABBIT

How to sign it
With your index and middle fingers make 'rabbit ears' on your head, just twitching them forward slightly.

SHEEP

How to sign it
With your little fingers, mime curly horns coming out from your temples.

Animal and vehicle signs are not only great fun, they also encourage your baby to play around with the sounds which are the building blocks of future speech. You may not be keen to call a 'sheep' a 'baa baa' or to call an 'aeroplane' a 'neeowww', but sounds such as these are wonderful practice for those little mouths getting around the speech sounds they will soon be using. We will cover speech sounds in more detail in Chapter 07.

If animals aren't a firm favourite with your child, then you may find that vehicles might be something that captivates their attention. Boys in particular seem to love anything that moves or has wheels.

> **REMEMBER:** Your child will want to tell you about things in his world that interests him – whether that be visual or audible. It may well be things that as adults we take for granted or just no longer see or hear. Children are often more perceptive and as the old saying goes, try to 'see things through a child's eyes'.

If your child is fascinated by moving parts – bikes, cars, trains etc. – then the following signs are ones you might find particularly helpful.

TRAIN

How to sign it
With arms bent and fists clenched at your sides, mime train wheels and say 'train'.

figure 25 train

CAR

How to sign it

With hands in front of you, mime a small steering wheel.

BOAT

How to sign it

Touch your finger tips together, palms facing inwards but apart, so you are making a boat's 'bow' shape. Move your boat shape forward, saying 'boat'.

figure 26 boat

AEROPLANE

How to sign it

Make a fist and then have your thumb and little finger sticking out as if they are wings. You can then move your 'plane' through the sky, making the appropriate 'neeeooooowwww' sound!

When Helen and her daughter were playing out in the garden Eloise spotted an aeroplane and so her mum naturally signed 'plane' to her – then a bird flew by and Eloise signed 'bird' to her mum, then when she realized nothing else was flying by she signed and said 'more' mummy. Helen found it hilarious that her daughter thought she could control the fly-bys! A classic moment when you wish you'd had the camcorder running. Signing gives you so much more insight into your child's world and their character at a much earlier age than may otherwise have been possible.

More useful signs

Dangerous, hot, cold, look, naughty, gentle, now, quick, what, careful, play/toys

So far we have covered some early basic signs that you can use many times in a day and will give you lots of practice in signing with your baby. We have also covered signs that babies find motivating and are often amongst the first signs they will use. We will now progress onto some signs which you as a parent or carer might find really helpful when communicating with your child. These are amongst some of the most common signs parents will ask for. It is worth noting, at this point, that these are generally not signs babies will tend to use early on, but you will be amazed at how many babies from 1 year onwards will use some or all of these signs.

When your baby gets a little more active, their modest world suddenly opens up to them. From being a small baby who will sit and play beautifully with a selection of toys, suddenly they quickly seem able to crawl or maybe bottom shuffle and then walk. Favourite ornaments are hastily removed, certain cupboard doors may be child-proofed (and sometimes adult-proofed!) and, for some, this is when the grey hairs begin to appear as you try and maintain a safe and stimulating environment for your baby.

Before we even had Sasha, my husband began to worry about having a baby in the house and his precious speakers. Since Sasha started crawling, the 'no' sign has been invaluable, especially regarding Daddy's speakers and other gadgets. She will crawl up to them and then sign 'no' and now says 'no, no, no' at the same time. She knows exactly what she can and can't touch and we don't need to keep repeating ourselves.

Angie Duckett

If your child is heading towards something hazardous, reaching out to touch, or putting themselves into a potentially dangerous situation, you may wish to continue to use the 'stop', or 'no' sign, each of which would be equally valid. However, as you are aware, it is so important to immerse children in language, and as they get older you may wish to use different words and signs, whilst keeping the message the same. 'Dangerous' can provide a great alternative.

DANGEROUS

How to sign it

Start with your index finger touching between your eyes. Use a straight hand, facing sideways. Start between your eyes and move down strongly in an arc, saying 'dangerous'.

figure 27 dangerous

When to use it

As your baby gets older and begins walking, you can use the 'dangerous' sign many times during the day. When outside you can use this sign near the roads, in conjunction with the 'wait' and 'stop' signs.

As parents with young children, we aim to provide a safe home environment for them, however, you may find your family and friends' houses are not quite so baby friendly. Anything electrical or mechanical seems to hold a special fascination for the boys, and for some the fireplace also seems to be a great place to explore. Using the 'dangerous' sign might be one that becomes extremely evident within your signing vocabulary, and don't forget it will often be used in conjunction with the 'no' or 'don't touch' signs too.

HOT

As you can imagine, 'hot' is a particularly useful sign for your young baby to learn, and again is often used in conjunction with the 'don't touch'/'no' or even 'dangerous' signs – all of which we have previously covered. 'Hot' is such an easy sign to learn and use, and it's very expressive too.

How to sign it
With five fingers spread apart, quickly touch your fingers to your lips and then withdraw them – saying 'hot'.

figure 28 hot

> *Will had been using signs at home but he hadn't really used them around people he didn't know. Shortly after Will's first birthday we were at a restaurant for a family meal. He crawled over to a bar area that had spot lights mounted into a foot rest, he pulled himself up to stand near a light, he turned round and signed 'hot' to the waitress! I couldn't believe it. He was getting more and more confident every day. I told the waitress what he was saying and she was amazed. This baby knew the lights were hot and he told us even though he couldn't talk.*
>
> Kathryn Furber

When to use it
To try to help your child learn and understand the concept of 'hot' you may wish to use a recently finished hot drink and gently place their hand on the edge of the warm cup and sign 'hot'. You can follow this with the 'don't touch' ('no') sign.

WARNING: Although your baby may understand the concept of 'hot' please continue to ensure that hot drinks and any other hot objects are well away from baby's reach or otherwise protected.

Another time to use the 'hot' sign is during dinner, especially if you are waiting for your child's dinner to cool down. If this is the case, let your child know their dinner is 'hot' – again you may wish to carefully place their hand on the side of the bowl, and sign 'hot'. You may then wish to let your child know they need to 'wait', using the 'wait' sign (holding both hands in the air, as if you are saying 'stop' – see page 96 for a full description). This will not only enable your child to help grasp the concept of why he/she needs to wait for their dinner, it will also help them comprehend the concept of what the word 'hot' means.

When your child can sign these important messages to you, you will finally realize that they comprehend what you are saying, and by using signing, they can communicate their understanding to you. Bear in mind your baby can be signing these concepts long before they are talking.

Mariette and I have been signing since she was 11 months old. We joined a signing class to help us to learn and to have some fun socializing too. Mariette very quickly learnt the 'hot' sign (very handy for obvious reasons) and 'finished', which was brilliant as it stopped her from throwing her food bowl across the room when she didn't want to eat any more! Also from a safety point of view, for example, 'stop', 'hot' and 'pain' were all really useful signs. We have found signing invaluable as it has lowered the number of tantrums she was having!

Elizabeth Nurse

COLD

How to sign it
Clench your fists directly in front of your chest, then in small movements shake them up and down, as if you were miming a 'Brrrr!'

When to use it

Working along the same lines as 'hot', an easy way to introduce the 'cold' sign to your baby is with a pack of frozen peas carefully wrapped in a tea-towel. By placing their hand briefly on the cold peas this can make the word 'cold' go from an obscure word to an understandable concept. For example, if you have a child who doesn't like to put their coat on, by helping them to understand the reason why it is important, i.e. it's cold outside, you are hopefully a little closer to your child wanting to do it more willingly. You may be surprised that sometimes just a quick explanation can be all the incentive a child needs.

> *My daughter Gabrielle would sign to me at bedtime whether her milk was too hot or cold enabling me to settle her very quickly at bedtime.*
>
> Michelle Elmer

It is amazing at how quickly babies can understand a sign, and transfer that knowledge into different situations and scenarios. I can remember one parent telling me she had entered her daughter's bedroom in the night as she was crying. After checking her daughters' nappy, and making sure she wasn't thirsty, she asked her daughter what the matter was, her daughter signed 'cold'. She had only taught her the sign two weeks previously.

By giving your baby a whole range of signs relevant to their world, you are giving them many opportunities to communicate in ways that you may not have thought possible. Included throughout this book are real-life illustrations of situations where parents have used the various signs described. This is deliberate in the hope that it will continue to inspire you to use as many signs as you can remember with your child. Nevertheless, don't get too carried away with your signing and forget the golden rule of only signing one word per sentence to your child.

NAUGHTY

How to sign it

With a clenched fist in front of you, raise your little finger.

When to use it

At this point it is worth noting the importance of labelling your child's *behaviour* as naughty, rather than labelling them as a person as naughty. For example, 'Don't throw your food on the floor – that's naughty' would be a way to label the behaviour, or you may wish to limit it further and just say 'No, naughty', rather than use an inappropriate phrase such as 'You naughty boy'.

GENTLE

Gentle is a lovely model of behaviour and something that we wish our children would always display around others, and especially with younger babies. It seems that some children right from birth are naturally very soft and gentle, and continue throughout their lives to be so. However, it appears that the majority of children at some point in their early lives, usually around the age of 2, will go through a stage of being less than gentle with younger babies, animals etc. Some will just have a natural, almost idle curiosity, and so, on occasion, just want to find out what does happen when you pull at the little baby, or yank the cat's tail.

The sign to use for 'gentle' is a great sign and is one that is very effective whether you are right next to your child or, if they are more familiar with it, from across the other side of a room. It is a very expressive sign, and when you use it you may find that your voice softens, and naturally becomes lower and slower.

How to sign it

With one hand, slowly and gently stroke the back of your other hand, remembering to say the word 'gentle' at the same time.

figure 29 gentle

When to use it

'Gentle' is actually quite a difficult concept to try and explain to a child and can often be misunderstood. The reason a child can misunderstand the word is the way that we, as adults, tend to use it when our children are actually being rough – so when tugging at another child, we will say 'be gentle'. This can give them mixed messages if they haven't fully understood what 'gentle' means.

One way to try and avoid the above scenario and give your child the correct meaning for the word 'gentle', is to take their hand and gently stroke a baby's hand, arm, leg, tummy, constantly saying 'gentle' – you can then proceed to show them the sign. As much as possible it is better to try and use the word in a positive context like this, before using it to show them the behaviour that you would like to see if they are being too rough.

WHAT?

This is a sign that you may find you actually begin to use quite a lot. '*What* is it?', '*What* do you want?' How many times is your baby crying, pointing, trying to talk or doing something that you don't understand? Every child will go through the baby babble stage. They are trying to make sense of their world and relating it to us in 'baby talk'. Most times we are totally ignorant of 'conversations' they are engaging in with us. The frustration for some babies is very apparent. Signing at least gives your child the opportunity to tell you what the problem is.

How to sign it

Wave your index finger from side to side.

When to use it

Next time your child is trying to 'tell' you something, demanding that you understand, why not try using the 'what' sign? You may find that this stops your child in their tracks (especially if they are crying). Your child will know they are getting your attention and it provides them with the opportunity to 'tell' you what the problem is.

When asking '*What* do you want?', you may wish to give them some prompts, i.e. 'Would you like a *drink*?', using the sign and, if their drink is handy, holding that up too. If that clearly isn't the answer, you can sign 'no' and try something else. Once you know what it is they are after, don't forget to show them the sign, and say the word. It won't be long before your child learns the signs for the things that are important to them and thereby limiting the times you may have to guess what it is your child wants.

LOOK

On the surface you may think this is a sign you won't use very often, but you may be surprised at how incredibly useful it can be.

How to sign it

Using your index finger (as if pointing to your eye) swiftly move it away in the direction of where you are indicating to your child to look.

When to use it

With a child that needs instruction, or indeed to be told how loved they are, you can ask your child to 'look' at you – this is a great sign to use to achieve eye contact with your child. Alternatively, if you are trying to show your child a new object or a bird in a tree, you can use the 'look' sign.

NOW

This may not be a sign that you use when you are beginning to sign with a young baby, but is extremely useful with a toddler, especially one that might have a strong will of their own! 'Now' is a great sign that lets your hands do the talking for you.

How to sign it

Start with your palms facing upwards and your fingertips facing in at chest level, then make one strong movement down to waist level. Remember to say 'now'.

figure 30 now

When to use it

I have noticed parents using this sign across the playground with primary aged children, asking their child to come 'now' – again letting their hands rather than their voice do the shouting.

QUICK/HURRY UP

How to sign it

Index finger quickly strikes the side of the other index finger.

When to use it

This is another sign that goes hand in hand with the 'now' sign, and is used in similar circumstances. You can also use this sign to play games with your child, alternating between fast/quick and slow.

CAREFUL

How to sign it

With your thumb and index finger, form the letter 'C'. Move two 'c' shaped hands down and out from your eyes, saying 'careful'.

figure 31 careful

When to use it

Careful is such a valuable sign, that you can use in a variety of circumstances; you may find you use it with early walkers, or boisterous boys who love to climb, or even a young child holding a pet or a new baby. You will find this often goes hand in hand with the 'gentle' sign shown on page 76.

PLAY/TOYS

How to sign it

With flat hands, make small upward moving circles in front of you, rotating your wrists and saying 'play'.

figure 32 play/toys

When to use it

You can use this any time you reach for the toy box at home. Alternatively you may wish to use this sign when you go to playgroup or a parent and toddler environment to signify going to play with the toys.

> **REMEMBER:** Your baby can comprehend what you are saying, and through signing can communicate their understanding to you long before they are able to talk.

At this point in the book you should have a good understanding of what baby signing is and how to incorporate some of the signs into your daily life. Many of the routines you and your baby will go through each day have been covered so far, with many additional motivating signs included to enable you to show your baby the signs for things that relate directly to their world.

04

emotional development

In this chapter you will learn:
- the importance of labelling your child's emotions
- signs to use to help your child in their emotional development.

Emotions – how does your baby feel?

Signs for feelings are very valuable for babies, although hugely under-estimated. Fortunately for parents, emotions are very easily revealed to parents of young babies; they don't ever try to hide them as we might as adults. They are open books in that respect, and we can read them well. When they are tired they will often begin by rubbing their eyes, or yawning – catching these cues early, you can easily show your baby the appropriate sign, and then put them straight down for a sleep. Missing that early cue will often result in a crying baby who can be much harder to settle. When they are happy or find something or someone funny, they will naturally begin laughing. However, if they are angry, sad, tired, frightened or in pain, they may cry and you may not be sure which emotion they are expressing. Emotional development is often something that can be seriously understated when dealing with babies and toddlers, despite that being a primary feature in their life. Much of a baby's world revolves around their emotions.

Anna told me her daughter was 16 months old when she saw her friend in a stripy black and white jumper. Her daughter immediately started laughing, and signing 'zebra'!

The above is such a wonderful example of how we can see a baby's or toddler's personality and sense of humour developing, and through signing giving them a great opportunity in which they can share it with us. No longer are you left to guess the source of your child's pleasure. When they can point and sign the source of their amusement – a 'zebra' sign on observing a stripy jumper, for example – you will enjoy a mutually rewarding exchange.

HAPPY

How to sign it
Keep left cupped hand still, then rub right cupped hand from index finder out to thumb. Rub cupped hands with glee.

figure 33 happy

SAD

How to sign it
Flat hand (facing sideways, fingertips up) moves down the middle of your face.

When to use it
When your baby is 'angry', 'sad', 'tired' or 'frightened' try showing empathy and understanding by labelling such emotions with signs. Offering labels in this way can comfort those feelings beyond your baby's control and lead to supporting benefits in emotional development.

LAUGH/FUNNY

How to sign it
Make a 'c' with index finger and thumb, and move up and down in front of your jaw, as if you are miming jaw moving up and down with laughter.

TIRED

How to sign it
A really natural sign – with a clenched hand, rub your eyes.

FRIGHTENED

How to sign it
Clawed hand trembles in front of your chest.

When to use it
It can often be the strangest things that frighten children, some of which may seem quite bizarre to us. Many children, for example, can be frightened by clowns, or people dressed up in large animal suits. Numerous images on the television can be too much for your young child to comprehend. Your child will not know or be able to verbalize this strange feeling within. However, they will know that they desperately need the comfort and safety of mum or dad. You can use this opportunity to show your child the frightened sign as described above, and where appropriate gently show your child the frightening object – showing them that it is not something they need to be fearful of.

ANGRY

How to sign it
Clawed hands, with palms facing you, make small movements alternating up and down.

figure 34 angry

For many adults, labelling feelings can seem a little bit of a strange concept, and an area that can provoke a few questions: Do I really want to show my child the angry sign, when I want them to be calm and loving? Will showing them such signs not make my child angrier?

You will be showing your child these signs in context, so therefore your child will already be feeling these emotions, but may not necessarily understand the depth or breath of emotions within. By giving your child a sign for these emotions, you are also showing a deep level of understanding with your child. Therefore this range of signs can help babies cope with strong emotions and feel understood.

Toddlers who are familiar with the 'angry' sign will often use it themselves to channel their frustration. It is a very descriptive sign for how your baby is feeling when they have 'lost it'. Many 2-year-olds who signed as babies will still use this sign to show frustration when deeply upset. It is far better to use such a sign than thrashing out. This is a sign that can be very useful to use even when your child is able to say the word, as it is such a descriptive sign.

> **Top tip**
>
> Try and keep using the signs for emotions even when words come.

Why does my child often seem frustrated?

A pre-verbal child will often be frustrated from not being understood, and therefore his or her needs not being met. Parents of signing children will often comment that signing has reduced frustration and temper tantrums in their children. In some children, signing has proven to almost eliminate tantrums completely! For those who still succumb to them, it has been reported that it is predominately due to being told 'no' rather than from the frustration of not being understood. Unfortunately, we will always be setting boundaries for our children, so for those stronger-willed children, signing can play a significant role, but those tantrums, although reduced, may continue when limits are set and enforced with them.

I have observed some babies who really thought they could talk, and yet we as adults would be hearing 'double dutch'. At this point, children can get very frustrated when they are urgently trying to tell you something. They may repeat their utterance twice or maybe three times, almost begging you to understand their baby babble. I would suggest that you use this opportunity to give your child good eye contact, and ask your child to 'sign' it to you as well. It is then that you will finally be able to understand what they are trying to communicate with you. Each time this happens, try to use the opportunity to reiterate the word they have been so desperately been trying to form. Get them to copy it and repeat it back to you if you can. In the early stages it is likely to be far from perfect and intelligible, but next time at least you may have an idea what '*&%\$>!sh' is!

Included below is a case study of a mum and her son who often appeared angry and frustrated. You will notice how Jane, the mum, appropriately uses the 'angry' sign with her strong-willed son. This will hopefully give you more insight into what effect this can have on your child when you help them by labelling feelings.

Case study

As Jayden was quite poorly from a very young baby, he had to undergo numerous tests, even at 2 weeks old he underwent a lumbar puncture. From an early age, with constant admissions to hospital, his experience was that people hurt him, things and food that went in his mouth hurt him etc. He always seemed a bit 'different' from other children. He certainly wasn't very social, and was often very tetchy and angry. Around a year old, I can remember thinking, my goodness, if my son is like this at 1, what on earth will he be like at 2? (The terrible twos by then was an alarming thought, with a wild 1-year-old!) He is a strong-willed boy, but then that's hardly surprising as quite a few times he has had to fight for his very existence. Although we were aware of what he had gone through, and this had given a little justification for how he was, it still wasn't too much comfort when it is your 13-month-old having a huge tantrum! It was then that we began to use more of the feelings signs we had been taught, especially the 'angry' sign. It was incredible. When we started to give him a label for his feelings, and show him we understood what he was experiencing, he really calmed down. I was able to empathize, and let him know I understood he was angry (even though I didn't always understand why). It was as if by recognizing and acknowledging his feelings he felt like he didn't need to fight so hard, he would then often soften towards me, and allow me to comfort him. I cannot tell you what a breakthrough that was for us as a family.

Jane and Jayden

Singing is a great way of releasing emotion and expressing yourself. Try singing this to the tune of 'If you're happy and you know it', it's great for teaching your child about emotions.

♪

'If you're *angry* and you know it stamp your feet!
If you're *angry* and you know it stamp your feet!
If you're *angry* and you know it
and you really want to show it
If you're *angry* and you know it stamp your feet'

♪

Other verses can include:

- If you're naughty and you know it say you're sorry.
- If you're tired and you know it go to sleep.
- If you're sad and you know it have a cry.
- If you're frightened and you know it have a cuddle.

The list can continue as long as your imagination allows.

Pain and medicine

'Pain' may not be a sign you may initially think of using with a baby, unless of course they have particular health issues. However, think of a 6-month-old trying to sit up for the first time who keeps falling over; a 9-month-old standing, holding onto furniture who loses their balance; a 13-month-old taking their first steps before becoming unsteady on their feet; the 18-month-old who is trying out stairs for the first time; the 2-year-old who is running too fast – these are just simple everyday occurrences in your baby's life where the pain sign can easily be implemented.

PAIN/HURT

How to sign it
With both index fingers pointing together – keep prodding them both together.

figure 35 pain

When to use it

Somewhere around the age of 6 months, a baby's first two lower front teeth will begin to poke through their gums – for most this will cause varying degrees of pain and discomfort. If you know this is the reason your baby may be fussing or crying, use the pain sign, near the mouth or gum area. For some babies a more concrete and immediate use of the sign is beneficial, so also use the pain sign anytime your baby falls over and bumps themselves.

You never know how showing your baby these useful signs will impact on your family, or indeed how your child may come to use them, as Martin discovered with his eldest son:

Case study

I thought learning to use the pain and feeling signs was a little odd for such young babies, but didn't realize how useful these would become to us. I had been told how to use the pain sign, and initially began using it whenever he fell over and bumped himself. A few months after learning them, I put my son to bed, and he began crying. I went in, said 'ssshhhh, ssshh', told him to go to sleep and went out again. He continued crying. I went back in again after a few minutes, checked his nappy, made sure he wasn't too hot etc., settled him down again, and left the room. The third time, I just lay him down again and walked out (I knew he wasn't hungry, he had recently had his milk). I couldn't perceive any reason for the crying – I wanted him to know I was still around, but I also wanted him to know this was the time for him to sleep. The fifth time of going in and out, I turned to him and said '*What* is it? *What*'s the matter?' (signing 'what'). Of course I didn't expect any response from him, after all he couldn't talk... He sat there crying and then signed 'pain'. I was astounded. It would never have entered my head that his continual crying was because he was in pain. I had just thought he didn't want to go to sleep, and was protesting about being put in his bed. My natural instinct if the crying had continued would be to sit next to his cot, as a presence for him, until he settled. Giving him medicine wouldn't have occurred to me as it wasn't the high-pitched pain cry he had when he fell over etc. I couldn't believe I would never have known he was in pain, if he wasn't able to sign to me. I immediately picked him up, cuddled him and gave him Calpol. Within half an hour he had settled.

After this 'successful' attempt at using this sign, we found he was using it more regularly, often a little while after dinner. It later transpired he had food allergies and was even intolerant to the soya milk the hospital had given him. Even now, if he has foods he is allergic to, he will get stomach cramps, diarrhoea etc., but we had no idea initially he was experiencing all this as a baby too. It is times like this when again signing has been invaluable for us as a family, allowing us to appropriately respond to our children, and giving them a way to effectively communicate to us.

Martin

Try signing 'pain' whenever your baby bumps or hurts themselves this week. Many babies respond very well to this sign and can begin to use it appropriately themselves. Teething is something that every baby goes through with varying degrees of distress. Jess was a very bright little girl and at around 15-months-old was frequently putting a few signs together – therefore signing in sentences. She would often sign 'pain' to her mum Joanne, point to her teeth, then 'medicine' and 'more' – an incredibly clear indication of what she needed! At 15 months Jess was extremely articulate in what her wishes were, and what she needed to alleviate her discomfort.

Top tip

When using the pain sign with your child, use it to indicate the area that is hurting, i.e. knee, tummy, teeth. When your child uses it for themselves they can show you what or where in their body they are hurting.

MEDICINE

How to sign it

Make a loosely held fist with your left hand, then with the little finger tip of your right hand trace around the top of the fist – as if tracing the opening of a small jar.

figure 36 medicine

When to use it

If your child has a high temperature, requires regular medication or you feel needs Calpol or even teething gel, try and use this sign before administering medication to your baby.

DOCTOR

How to sign it

With thumb and index finger, place on edge of wrist (as if taking a pulse).

For most non-signing babies, parents can only begin to guess at what may be causing their baby to be unsettled. With signing babies we can only make educated guesses at what the positive benefits are to our child when they are understood, as well as having the ability to communicate to us. The expectation is that it can only positively impact on their confidence, self-esteem and emotional development.

Tahlia's first signs were 'where' and 'hurt' (she had to go to hospital for five weeks for surgery when she was 1 year-old and has since had several medical treatments). She then quickly progressed to 'Mummy' (using one instead of three fingers), 'no' (which she also uses for 'finished'), 'change nappy' (also pointing to her bum!) and 'butterfly'. She is now 18 months old and in the last few weeks we've seen an explosion of signs from Tahlia. It's as though she's slowly been absorbing them and is now ready to talk fluently with her hands as well as her voice – albeit still in her own language most of the time! We can tell she gets a lot of satisfaction from the fact that we understand her so much better, and praise her so much when she signs and speaks. Interestingly she doesn't sign much in class or when she watches the Sing and Sign DVD, but does more and more the rest of the time.

Alison Lovegrove

Love and manners

'I love you' is a wonderful sign to share, either as three separate signs or just as the single 'love' sign, which is simpler for younger babies to grasp.

LOVE

How to sign it
Two hands cross lovingly across your chest

When to use it
This sign in particular is one that can last for years, and can be great to use across a crowded room.

PLEASE

How to sign it

With a flat hand on your chin, fingertips pointing up, palm towards you, move your hand out and down from your chin in a large arc.

figure 37 please

When to use it

When you are just setting out with signing, and your baby may only be around 6 months old, the signs for 'please' and 'thank you' aren't ones to place too heavy an importance on as first signs, as these tend to be words that delight parents, rather than words that make babies happy. Early signs therefore should be words that babies really want to say. Inspiring communication is so much more fun than requesting it.

Conversely, slightly older babies are more prepared for the niceties of manners and politeness and therefore 'please' and 'thank you' begin to be attractive signs to encourage and use more and more in your daily signing. Most parents are delighted when their child learns the art of good manners before being able to speak.

Top tip

Parents can sometimes get confused between the 'please' and 'thank you' signs as one is a longer gesture of the other. When signing 'please' think 'Please to your knees' as it is a larger gesture than 'thank you'.

THANK YOU

How to sign it

With a flat hand on your chin, fingertips pointing up, palm towards you. Move your fingertips out and down from your chin in a small static movement that should finish about 10–15cm from your face.

figure 38 thank you

When to use it

When teaching a child to be appreciative, some parents will start with trying to get their child to say 'ta' whilst others will only use 'thank you'. This is a purely individual choice and the sign will remain the same even if you progress from 'ta' to 'thank you'. Babies find 'ta' an easier word to say, whilst 'thank you' babies will tend to mimic the intonation in your voice rather than repeating the actual word. Both can be pleasing to parents, especially when accompanied by the sign.

Top tip

Continue to use the 'thank you' sign with your child even when they are able to say the word. You will find there will be many occasions when even a primary school aged child will forget to say 'thank you'. You can silently prompt them with the 'thank you' sign, and make your child appear to have excellent manners.

SORRY

Even if your baby is starting to talk now, there are likely to be some favourite signs which stay around for a while. Some signs are particularly recommended to continue using, even if your baby is saying them. 'Sorry' is one such word.

How to sign it

Make a fist, and rub a small circle in the middle of your chest.

figure 39 sorry

When to use it

Sometimes babies are just too ashamed (or even too proud!) to say the word, so rather than have a stand-off, which can end up being distressing for everyone, the sorry sign can offer a shy apology. You can also use this gesture to prompt your child to say sorry.

SHARE

All of us want our children to be caring, sharing individuals who are readily willing to share their toys. The reality is that many children, especially toddlers, become very territorial and some, just for a short time, obtain a massive sense of ownership and can become unwilling to relinquish or share property. This is largely due to a young child not being able to understand the idea that something given up now can be retrieved later, also patience is in short supply at this age.

How to sign it
Mime 'give' and 'take' with both hands, palms faced upwards.

figure 40 share

When to use it
As much as possible, it is always advisable to put a positive slant on things, but most children will perceive sharing as having to surrender a favourite toy or possession. One way to turn this on its head is to make sharing an enjoyable experience for your child by using, for example, a favourite food. If you are sitting down giving your child a snack of bread and you sit down with their favourite food, it is highly likely they will be pointing, grabbing or doing anything to get their favourite food from your plate. You can use this opportunity to show them the 'share' sign, maybe saying a phrase such as 'Mummy *share* her strawberries with you?' This also works very well when turned into a game with a favourite toy, teaching your child to take turns and 'share'. Giving your child this opportunity to share in

a non-threatening environment, enables you to appropriately judge the time to 'share' it back again. Learning in this way gives your child a head start when it comes to sharing amongst friends of their own age.

WAIT

How to sign it

Put both hands in front of your body, hands flat, palms outwards, move your hands purposefully down in front of you.

figure 41 wait

When to use it

This can be an incredibly useful sign in a variety of circumstances – a child pulling at your leg when you are paying for goods, whilst waiting to cross the road, or a child desperate for food that is cooling. As your child gets older and they want to interrupt you, you can allow your hands do the talking, asking them to wait until you are finished. 'Wait' is a very simple sign that holds a strong message.

By using the signs for emotions, signs for when your child is in pain or discomfort, as well as those all important signs associated with manners, you will be able to engage with your child on a level that simply was not possible before. You will be able to enter their world, one that is smothered in emotions, and begin to show empathy with them by labelling their emotions with signs or by acknowledging their pain. The benefits of using these signs cannot be underestimated.

05

encouraging signing with children at home and in childcare

In this chapter you will learn:
- creative ways to sign for important people in your life
- how to maintain signing if your child is at nursery or daycare
- effective communication with a child in a bilingual family.

Important people in your baby's world

By using signs for the names of favourite friends and relatives, you can enrich your baby's excitement and anticipation at seeing them. You can choose the signs listed here or you can be inventive, creating gestures that indicate personal characteristics such as glasses or a beard – maybe you have a family member who is particularly clever, the sign for which is dragging a thumb horizontally across your forehead – or you could use the sign for an initial letter of a person's name (see the alphabet on the Sing and Sign CD). Your baby will not yet have the fine motor control to form some letter shapes accurately but this does not matter. Be accurate yourself and let your baby approximate at this stage.

MUMMY

How to sign it
Index, middle and ring fingers tap twice on the opposite palm.

DADDY

How to sign it
Closed index and middle finger tap twice on the closed index and middle finger of the opposite hand.

Don't forget those oh-so motivating characters like Noddy, Teletubbies, Fimbles etc. Remember… What does your baby want to talk about? What is important in their world? Be imaginative in creating signs for your baby.

Baby signing is wonderful fun for all the family; older siblings love it. They often master signs quickly and adore this 'special' communication with their little brother or sister.

BROTHER

How to sign it

Make a fist, with thumbs up, knuckles inwards, rub up and down.

figure 42 brother

SISTER

How to sign it

Hooked index finger taps the bridge of your nose twice.

When to use it

If your baby has an older brother or sister, you can use these signs any time you use their name. However, if they have more than one brother or more than one sister, you will have to be inventive, and create a sign for additional siblings – maybe one loves to sing, so you could mime a microphone in front of your mouth, or another has long hair, so you could mime that. Alternatively, you may like to use the boy/girl signs for additional siblings.

BOY

How to sign it

Index finger sweeps under your chin from left to right.

GIRL

How to sign it

Index finger makes two small strokes down from your cheek towards your mouth.

Some grandparents will want to participate in every area of their grandchild's development, others can be skeptical at first of what they may see as 'a new fad of the modern age'. However, once a baby starts signing and begins to communicate, it can be amazing how many initial skeptics change their minds!

GRANDAD/GRANDPA etc.

How to sign it

With fingers spread apart, hand sideways on, put the tip of your thumb on your forehead, and moving your hand forwards and down making small arcs in front of you.

figure 43 grandad

GRANDMA/NANNA etc.

How to sign it

With fingers spread, hand facing sideways, make small arc movements down from your chin.

Top tip

As the signs for Grandma and Grandad are similar, here is a top tip to help you remember which way round to sign them: Grandad is a thinker – so comes down from his head, Grandma is a talker – so the sign comes down from her chin!

Below are a few additional signs that you might find helpful for special people in your baby's life.

AUNTIE

How to sign it
With index and middle finger bent and slightly apart, tap your chin.

UNCLE

How to sign it
Index finger brushes back of other little finger twice.

COUSIN

How to sign it
Make a 'c' shape with your thumb and forefinger, brush this twice under your chin.

FRIEND

How to sign it
Clasp one hand with the other – as if shaking hands – mime this up and down.

figure 44 friend

Baby's own picture book

You may be surprised at how many babies appreciate having a personal special friends and family picture book. For many this will become their most treasured possession. Use a simple slip-in photo album, and either print off additional photos of friends and family, or merely use photos that you may have put aside for a variety of reasons – perhaps use those that were just not good enough for your 'official' family album.

Some families can be quite complex in the number of grandparents they have, so using photos to differentiate between Granddad, Grandpa and Grandpops, for example, can be a great way to help your child use an appropriate sign for the right person. This has the added advantage of giving you more opportunity to use the sign and word other than just when the person comes to visit. Using a photo album to help reinforce the signs will also benefit your child with extra practice in trying to say the words. You may not find it too long before your baby is trying to say the words of friends and family and dropping the signs altogether – a delight for any grandparent to hear their name being spoken.

> **REMEMBER:** Babies will sign and say words for things that interest them, and undoubtedly people will feature highly on any baby's list.

So try it for yourself. An album of your baby's own can become a precious resource and makes lovely bedtime reading with plenty of opportunity to talk about loved ones and reinforce the signs which you may like to choose from some shown at the beginning of this chapter.

Signing in a nursery setting

If your baby spends some time in the care of others who may not use signs with them, don't let that give you an excuse to be inconsistent yourself. You are still probably spending more than enough time with your baby to make baby signing worthwhile. Morning and evening routines, a meal time or bathtime, all offer ideal opportunities to reinforce signs and can make your time together even more special. If whoever is looking after your child (nursery, child minder or grandparent) is happy to use a few signs too then that is a wonderful benefit. You can make it as easy as possible for them by printing out a page or two of your baby's favourite signs from the online dictionary on the website (**www.singandsign.com**) or by showing them the Sing and Sign DVD.

Many nurseries around the country understand the benefit, for staff and children, of adopting some simple signs as a part of the day's regular routines. This helps the children anticipate what will happen next, understand boundaries, and helps promote a calm atmosphere. Sing and Sign offers a Nursery Affiliation Programme and if your nursery would like to know more about how baby signing can help in childcare, please tell them to contact your Sing and Sign teacher or visit the Sing and Sign website.

> *We began signing with Isaac in Switzerland where he went to an all German-speaking crêche. We always spoke English at home. Once when I picked him up from the crêche he signed to me 'happy' and 'friends'. 'Friend' was our word for the crêche, so he was signing to me that he was happy at friends. This not only brought tears to my eyes (as one never really knows if one's baby is happy to go to crêche!), but it was the first time that he put two signs together!*
>
> Louise Joyce

In recent years there has been so much more research on how children learn and the different learning styles that can be adopted. The main classification systems that researchers have developed are: visual (seeing), auditory (hearing), kinaesthetic (moving) or tactile (touching) ways of learning.

Those who prefer a *visual* learning style:

- look at the teacher's face intently
- like looking at wall displays, books etc. and will recall information by remembering how it was set out on a page
- often recognize words by sight.

Those who prefer an *auditory* learning style:

- like the teacher to provide verbal instructions
- like dialogues, discussions and plays

- solve problems by talking about them
- use rhythm and sound as memory aids.

Those who prefer a *kinaesthetic* learning style:

- learn best when they are involved or active
- find it difficult to sit still for long periods
- use movement as a memory aid.

Those who have a *tactile* learning style:

- use writing and drawing as memory aids
- learn well in hands-on activities like projects and demonstrations.

By signing with your child, whether in a more formal nursery setting, or in the comfort of your own home, you are giving your child the opportunity to see, hear and do. Whenever they have a tough thing to learn – maybe they have trouble with their alphabet, or difficulty remembering a song, or there is a spelling they are stumbling over – signing can add an extra dimension to their learning. They hear what they are being told, but they also see it and are involved if they sign it themselves.

If you have a creative child who finds it a little difficult to 'tune in' to the logical brain processes often required in school learning, they will often excel at the more holistic approach that signing gives, thus also boosting their self-esteem. Using sign and speech together helps connections between their logical and creative thought processes.

I first heard about baby signing when I was working in a nursery in Bristol. Signing was used with some of the children, and we all found signing really fun and helpful. After starting in a new nanny job, I started to use a few of the signs that I remembered. It was surprising how fast the baby picked them up.

Kathryn Furber

Bilingual babies

Young children absorb everything they hear, see and feel and they keep it forever. The unique (pure) sounds of language are acquired with ease when learning during childhood, so by beginning to learn a second language early, children gain heaps of confidence and are able to learn correct pronunciation of different languages which can be extremely difficult to master at a later stage.

With a child who is not just learning a second language but is being brought up in a bilingual family, signing can be invaluable. Many bilingual children will begin to acquire speech a little later than children of the same age who are only being taught their mother tongue. Signing with a bilingual child helps the child to connect the two (or more) languages. The sign acts as an anchor for understanding the different languages. For example, if you point to a picture of a cow, and use the sign and say 'cow' in English and then use the same sign and say 'vaca', a toddler can easily understand that the sign stays the same whether you are speaking English or Spanish, therefore becoming the anchor for their understanding.

That very understanding will trigger the essential abstract thinking skills that are the basic tools for further learning.

I am Dutch and am bringing my kids up to be bilingual. This is the (maybe even the main) reason that I looked into baby signing, as I've always been told that bilingual kids tend to speak later because it takes that little bit longer to work the differences out, and I wanted a way to communicate with them whilst they were doing this. I started signing with my daughter when she was 6–7 months old, and she started to sign back to me at 11 months ('milk' was her first sign). Once she started she quickly learned other signs, and at 14 months (I'll always remember this), we were going to read a story, and I opened the cover of the book we were going to read. She then signed rabbit, and I was wondering why, as there weren't really any pictures or anything to be seen yet, or so I thought, because round the edge of the page was this tiny border with pictures that are important to a baby's world, amongst them a rabbit. This really brought home to me what great observers children are and how, where we tend to only see the big picture, they see all the small details first. Needless to say, my daughter started talking round about 18 months and has always been a great communicator in both English and Dutch (this is not just a proud mummy speaking as everyone including the health visitor has commented on this). I then continued to sign with her brother when he was born, and even though he started to sign later (at 14 months) and never used as many signs as his big sister (he did know them all as he has used them on occasion), at two he is now a very clear speaker too, and hardly ever stops (sometimes I wonder if I shouldn't have done the signing (GRIN)).

Being a bilingual family can be such fun – when either of my children would start telling me something, I wouldn't always know if they were talking English, Dutch or just baby babble. In those situations I found if I threw in a sign here and there, it could really clear things up.

Paula White

There is scientific evidence that children who are exposed to a second language from an early age not only achieve much better results in languages, but also in maths, science and music. It helps in general to build brainpower and cognitive skills. If you add signing into the equation, it enables clearer communication and clarity when you may not be sure what language your baby may be speaking.

Twins and multiple births

Multiple-birth parents are usually aware of the importance of helping each child develop their individuality while at the same time respecting the uniqueness of being a multiple. However, fostering individuality is easier said than done, and this also relates to acquiring language. You may have heard that multiple-birth children will often talk later than their single counterparts. However, multiples acquire language just as single-born children do, it's just that quite often they develop it at a slower pace. Even though multiples tend to make sounds and gestures early on to each other, they often say their first word (other than 'mama' or 'dada') about a month later than most single-born children. Language development, whether that be signing or speech, is a rewarding way to bring a closeness and intimacy with each other, as Helen describes with her twins in the following example.

> *Georgina had her favourite caterpillar glove puppet and was sitting close to Thomas who was playing with his dummy. Georgina turned around and Thomas reached forward and took her caterpillar. When Georgina looked back and saw it was gone she naturally looked at Thomas. Thomas smiled at her and signed 'gone' and 'where' and then laughed. He reached behind him and got the caterpillar and gave it a kiss (which Georgina likes to do). Thomas showed the caterpillar to Georgina and then hid it again and repeated the signs 'gone' and 'where' – they both laughed and Georgina signed 'more'. They played this game for about 5 minutes and it was so lovely to watch.*
>
> *When Thomas and Georgina were about 14 months old we were at The Mall in Bristol (a big shopping complex) and the children were looking around at things. Thomas tapped Georgina on the arm – as they were sitting side by side – and signed 'crocodile' to her. Then he called me and signed 'crocodile'. I couldn't see a crocodile anywhere and asked them both again. Thomas signed crocodile to Georgina again and she said 'des' ('yes'?) whilst looking at me and they both then pointed at the man, who was wearing a Lacoste emblem on his T-shirt.*
>
> Helen Hill

It is often reported that twins and children of multiple births will create a 'language' of words and sentences that only they can understand. In actual fact this is generally the use of immature or incorrect speech patterns, vocabulary or grammar when learning to talk. This is primarily due to multiples not having as many chances as single-born children to interact directly and individually with their parents. They will inevitably spend more time listening and communicating to each other than single-born children. Over time and during interaction with each other, words become warped, and speech is not being corrected in the same way it might be if you had a single baby. This phenomenon is sometimes known as 'twin-talk'. Up to half of twins who use twin talk will also have a speech and language difficulty. However, it is important to note, this may also be due to other factors, such as the fact that many twins or multiple births are often premature, which can provide its own challenges. For many parents of twins, this won't be an issue at all, but being aware of statistics such as these is often half the battle to avoiding them.

So if you are a parent of twins, how can you enhance your child's communication? To try and improve your babies' communication use as many signs as possible within your daily routines, but also try and schedule in as much individual time with your babies as possible – maybe by taking just one child shopping, taking the opportunity to slow your speech and give more eye contact to the one child. Within your daily schedule, such as changing nappies, use this time to give your baby one to one time where you might sing and use a lot of eye contact.

> I wasn't expecting to gain anything from baby signing, it was just something to do on a Wednesday morning involving singing and music with my twin girls. However, using signing has helped Ella, Freya, myself and our families to communicate with each other effectively and has dramatically reduced frustration through lack of understanding which has been so rewarding.
>
> Signing helped us in a situation with the youngest of our twins. It was about 5 months into the classes and Ella had been admitted into hospital with an infection and high temperature. The medical staff and I were trying to find out the cause of the illness and as Ella was only 11 months old she was unable to communicate verbally what the problem was. Ella was getting increasingly irritable and I continued to try and pacify her. I asked her on numerous occasions 'where does it hurt' but to no avail.
>
> Ella then caught my attention by using the sign for 'ouch/pain' near her stomach and then used the sign for 'drink' to indicate she was thirsty. She was given some water, drank it and then signed to me 'more', 'drink' and again did the 'ouch/pain' sign.
>
> I signed back to Ella to get a clearer understanding of what she was trying to tell me and she confirmed by signing it ('pain') again. The doctors were intrigued and asked what I was doing and I explained that we had been attending signing classes in Bristol and 'translated' what Ella was signing and requested that they check that specific area on her stomach. We subsequently found out that Ella had developed a urinary tract infection which needed specific treatment!
>
> Without baby signing it may have taken some time to find out what the problem was and caused Ella a lot more upset.
>
> Ella and Freya have grown and developed in their confidence and social interaction, and their speech has increased along with their

*enthusiasm for all things musical. I put this all down to the fun time
we have all had with Sing and Sign – we shall all really miss the
classes when we leave.*

Nayna Patel with Ella and Freya

Signing dads

The modern dad is generally considered to be different from
those a generation ago. Dads today are often perceived to have
a more active role in their child's life. With so many parents
going to work, many now do not have the luxury of attending
mid-week groups, and this would be especially true for dads.

The aim of this book is to bridge the gap for those parents who are
unable to attend such mid-week groups, and enable dads (or other
secondary carers) to learn the signs, thus providing continuity for
the child. This way all key people can be involved in actively
communicating with the child, before they are able to talk.

Not being a dad myself, I asked a couple of dads, both in
different situations, to tell you a little bit of their own experience
of baby signing. I have left this very much in their own words in
order for them to convey to you what they feel is important.

*Naturally as a parent you want the best for your child, you want to
understand their needs and give them the best possible start. For
me this was quite difficult as I was often at work during the day
whilst my wife was the main carer at home.*

*That said, when my boys were babies, signing became an
essential form of communication and allowed us to understand
their needs and them to understand us. The crying was often
eventually accompanied by a sign, so you then knew the reason
for the screams and weren't merely grasping the air in frustration
for answers.*

*My first experience of signing was coming in from work and seeing
my boys sitting in front of a video called 'Sing and Sign' and my
wife sitting with them talking and using exaggerated body
language and signs which they seemed to be attentive to. On the
video there were songs being accompanied by signing and my
eldest son transfixed to what was being communicated. Suddenly
a whole new world was being unravelled before me and I began to*

communicate with my son through signs I was learning from the video and more importantly those my wife was teaching me.

From something as simple as asking for food or milk to expressing a desire for 'more', it was amazing the amount of visual language my children picked up. Quite often signing became second nature particularly with my youngest son who was later diagnosed with a hearing loss.

There were certain times in the evening, after work, that I spent with the boys alone. For instance, at bathtime I found I could introduce signs I had been taught for certain toys like boats and signs for washing. At bedtime both my wife and I would read stories which were quite vocal, so more often than not the signing was accompanied by loud noises to complement the bedtime story.

The older my children became the more signs became second nature. It alleviated many temper tantrums as my sons could sign when asked what it was that was upsetting them. It is equally important for the parent who is not the primary carer to keep up the signing and give the child a level of consistency. In using signing it was important that my wife showed me the signs she had learned so that we were acting in the same way.

Lack of time is not an excuse for either parent: it will help you bond with your child and help to keep continuity in the family unit. I cannot advocate enough the benefits of signing which make the effort and time put in worthwhile.

Mick Melville-Reed, dad to Jacob, Joesph and baby Talitha

A father's role in signing

The term 'parenthood' is a problematic one to define because we all have differing experiences depending on who we are: whether we are mum or dad, whether we are the 'primary carer', or perhaps we work all week and only 'see the kids at the weekend'.

How does a dad's experience as a parent differ from that of a Mum's?

Who is the primary carer/secondary carer?

Who is at home? Who works elsewhere all day?

Some working/commuting dads only see kids at breakfast/bedtime/weekend...

If you are a dad, working all week, signing can therefore be a good way for you to 'catch up' by being involved in an established link between mum and baby.

<u>Why is it important for Dads to sign with their child</u>? – Signing can quickly become a common household language (not to sign would mean 'exclusion'), as well as giving 'continuity' between parents for the child.

Tabitha's vocabulary and sign repertoire was very large very early on – all children sign/walk/talk at different rates, but we felt Tabitha was definitely advantaged by word/sign stimulation early on.

<u>Major benefit of signing</u> – Signing alleviates frustration at not being understood – initially helps parent to 'underline' the meaning of a sentence with a simple sign; eventually the child learns to sign back and begins to discover the rewards of cross communication (i.e. getting what they are trying to ask for).

Later on, signing helps to communicate difficult sounding words when learning phonics and speech sounds – gives the child the confidence to attempt to pronounce the word because they have the sign to back up their intended meaning.

As Tabitha grew, signs fell away with progression of her speech – but with arrival of 'number two' (Tilly), Tabitha 'remembered' her old signing ways to communicate with her new sister.

Tilly was a typical 'second child' – she signed, walked and talked later because she liked to watch her older sibling do it all for her.

Christian Cotton, dad to Tabitha and Tilly

Both Mick and Christian have found signing with their children beneficial, and are pleased they took the time and effort to learn some simple signs. Time can play a large factor when choosing to sign with your baby. For most fathers, they might have an hour snatched before work, a few hours snatched after work and before bed, and then the so important weekends that form the primary time to be with their children.

REMEMBER: It cannot be overstated how spending small pieces of time learning signs and developing your repertoire will reap huge rewards when interacting with your baby.

Take a few moments to think about the time that you spend with your baby. What is it that you spend your time doing? Feeding? Playing? Bathing? Do you use the time to go out, or read to your child? Is there a particular routine that you follow? Maybe your special time with your baby is their night-time routine? Whatever it is, you should be able to find some signs throughout this book that you can incorporate into your individual time with your baby. Start with maybe two or three signs, and then add to them as you become more confident. You may be surprised at the positive difference this can make with your child, and improve your bond.

special needs

In this chapter you will learn:

- more about a few of the most common disabilities and disorders that affect children
- parents' accounts of how signing has helped their situation
- how to identify a particular difficulty and what to do.

This is such a complex area to deal with, but an area I certainly didn't want to ignore despite its complexities and the wide spectrum of disabilities and disorders. Signing programmes are regularly contacted by parents with babies and children who have Global Developmental Delay, Down Syndrome and hearing problems to name but a few. Quite often these children have already been diagnosed, and parents are enquiring as to whether signing will benefit their child. It is probably important to say at this point that **if you are at all concerned with your child's development or speech advancement, then it is always advisable to seek the advice of a health professional.**

Obviously all children, whether they have specialized needs or not, will naturally develop at different rates, and this rate will of course be further impacted upon by any other health implications there may be. You may well be reading this chapter as a parent of a child with special needs, wondering if signing will help your particular situation. Naturally it would be impossible to give an outright yes or no, but from experience (and you can read other parents' own experiences in this chapter), the overwhelming majority of parents will say yes!

This section explains and introduces a few of the most common needs that lead parents to enquire about baby signing, and includes the voices of 'experts' in the field – mothers and fathers who have had to deal with a variety of these issues with their children. If you are a parent of a child with special needs, I hope you find something here to help and inspire you.

Maia was born with Treacher Collins' Syndrome. Her ears are malformed yet she is able to hear well with her bone conductor hearing aid. She also has a tracheostomy to help her breathe and while this is in place she is unable to use her voice. Our motivation to use signing with Maia is twofold: we want to maximize her communication skills in light of both her hearing impairment and her temporary inability to speak; we imagine that signing will also support Maia's developing speech once the tracheostomy has been removed and we shall introduce Makaton signs (see Chapter 08) as she gets older.

We are certain that we would have begun using baby signing with a 'regular' baby as the benefits seem so great. With Maia, of course, it has been an important aspect of her upbringing from the earliest days and after months of singing and signing as often as *we could it is very exciting to embark on our first conversations. She is now 14 months old and has upward of 15 signs – which she is very proud of! Some signs are still rather approximate but she frequently uses them in the correct context. Interestingly, she is most consistent when prompted by the accompanying song and she often babbles with her hands as if in practice.*

We have no doubt that signing will ease Maia's frustration, develop her memory, help her confidence and increase her sensitivity towards non-verbal communication. Most importantly, for the time being, it is providing us with a great deal of fun and quality time together. We love the classes, and the warmth and understanding we have received from our teacher and classmates have helped us through this challenging year. It fills our hearts to see Maia making such enormous progress after her traumatic start to life. It is also of great comfort that baby signing is so popular and valued in the wider community. It has made the experience of having a hearing/voice-impaired child less isolating for us as we know that many parents and children are avid signers as well.

Josie and Martin Tollner with Maia aged 14 months

Developmental Delay

Parents often have concerns about their children's development, especially in a society when we seem to be constantly comparing our children, checking to see which children of the same age have attained a particular developmental milestone. This can cause a great deal of anxiety in parents, especially if your child still hasn't met the same milestone, possibly causing you to think that your child is a little 'slow' for their age or 'seems behind'. It is important to keep in mind that for each developmental milestone, there is a range of ages during which a child will normally meet it. For example, some children may walk as early as 9 months, while others may not walk until they are nearing 20 months old. Similarly, while there are those who seem to have nailed speech around 18 months and those who are still using very basic speech at a much later age, both can still be classed to be within 'normal' range.

Developmental Delay is usually a diagnosis made by a doctor based on strict guidelines. Usually when a child does not achieve one or more of their developmental milestones at the expected time, and it generally becomes an ongoing major delay in the process of their development, this is then called Developmental Delay. As developmental milestones are determined by the average age at which children attain each skill, not every child will reach them at the expected time. Statistically very few children will go on to be diagnosed with Developmental Delay or Global Developmental Delay. If your child is slightly or only temporarily lagging behind, that does not fall into the same category as Developmental Delay. Many children who fall into the second category will eventually develop normally over time, although maybe a little later than expected.

What causes Developmental Delay?

Developmental Delay can have many different causes, such as genetic causes (like Down Syndrome), or complications of pregnancy and birth (like prematurity or infections). Often, however, the specific cause is unknown. Some causes can be easily reversed if caught early enough, such as hearing loss from chronic ear infections, all of which I will try and cover to some degree in this chapter.

Delay can occur in one or many areas – for example, motor, language, social or thinking skills. Global Developmental Delay implies that the child has delays in all areas of development.

Although a doctor will diagnose the condition, it is usually you, the parent, that is the first to notice that your child may not be progressing at the same rate as other children the same age. It is vital that you talk with your doctor or health visitor about it. In some cases, this will be picked up at the regular developmental checks that our babies have. It will probably take several visits and possibly a referral to a developmental paediatric specialist to be sure that the delay is not just a temporary lag. Special testing can also help gauge your child's developmental level in relation to the developmental milestones.

Benefits of early diagnosis

Early developmental intervention and instruction helps to influence a young, impressionable and receptive brain. It helps to maximize a child's developmental potential, and their functional abilities such as social communication, mobility and adaptive skills. It can be really important for parents to learn what 'normal' development is, and how their child is developing in relation to that. They are then in a much better place to be able to tailor their expectations to what their particular child can achieve, and provide stimulation and toys to match the child's own individual developmental milestones.

We are now very aware that the first 3–5 years of a child's life are an amazing time of development, and that what happens during those years stays with a child for a lifetime. That's why it's so important to watch for signs of delays in development, and to get help from professionals if you suspect problems. The sooner a developmentally delayed child receives intervention, the better their progress will be.

> *While I was pregnant with Adam I had read about signing with babies and was very interested in it. It wasn't something I'd done with my other three children and so I thought I would give it a go!*
>
> *I have been attending signing classes since Adam was 7 months old – he is now nearly 2 and a half. At first I found it quite daunting trying to keep up and learn all these signs, but after a couple of weeks or so some started to sink in and the songs make them so much easier to learn! Adam was quite happy at this age to lie there and watch.*
>
> *As a few months passed, Adam's development was noticeably delayed. All the other babies were beginning to sign and as we progressed to the Improvers class some of them were saying words too – Adam was doing nothing. So we kept on going to the classes. We did three lots of Beginners and currently we are on our second Improvers! Earlier this year Adam finally did his first sign, which was 'duck', and has gone on to do a few more.*
>
> *Because of Adam's Global Development Delay, signing has been brilliant for him. He still can't say any words and so without the few signs he has learnt, communication would be very difficult.*
>
> *As Adam does have special needs, we have a lot of 'professionals' involved. I have had so much praise for introducing Adam to signing at such an early age and giving him a good head start.*
>
> Lisa Williamson

As we can see from Lisa's story, a developmental delay also impacted on the length of time it took for her son to learn to sign. Neverthelesss, signing can become a vital part of the learning process and enable communication when speech may be much further away.

Down Syndrome

It is often said that babies with Down Syndrome find it much harder to learn auditorily than they do visually, and with a large percentage of children with Down Syndrome having hearing problems, it therefore makes perfect sense to introduce signing alongside speech. Many children with Down Syndrome may have delayed speech with poor pronunciation, but depending on the severity of the condition, many will go on to intelligible speech. However, due to the low muscle tone of the face, smaller than average mouth cavity, and the shape and size of the tongue, speech does not generally come easily and quickly. Signing can be essential when trying to discriminate between similar-sounding words and sounds.

A few months after starting signing, Neve regularly used about 12 signs. We took her to visit my cousin who has Down Syndrome. They had disappeared behind a chair and were obviously playing together, when I noticed they were actually signing to one another. My cousin Stella, uses Makaton (see Chapter 08) to supplement her communication, and some of the Sing and Sign signs were recognizable to her!

Vanessa Kreimeia

My son Scott was born with Down Syndrome and we were told to sign to him from 6 months as we didn't realize how much his speech would be delayed. We began to learn Signalong when we moved back to Edinburgh and it was only after I had my second son Tom, that I found Sing and Sign. Scott is now aged 5 and at mainstream school. He still signs a lot and will sign 'cake' as we arrive at a party, 'horse' as we are getting ready for riding, and 'work' for daddy when he is at work, or 'plane' when he is down in London. Scott's speech is still delayed and he still gets Speech and Language therapy. He is beginning to use and understand pronouns, developing short sentences, understands turn taking and uses social words like sorry, excuse me, please and thank you.

He has done so well recognizing and saying the 7 jolly phonics sets but still has difficulty with C, K and G.

He still signs a lot, using a boardmarker for a picture timetable at home and school, and using symbols and gestures. He can recognize his name, mummy, daddy, his brother Tom, numbers

1–5 and can almost write his own name. His school and SLA and ASN teacher all say he is surpassing his IEP targets (individual education plan).

He has inspired us all to sign to each other when we are out of hearing distance. For example, when I am trying to get Graham or the boys' attention to come in for dinner, drink, tea etc. or when they are inside and I am out, or at the other end of the garden (we have 3 acres!) to convey what we want to say. Signing is now part of our lives and we don't know what we would do without it!

Caroline Forbes with Scott and Ben

Vanessa and Caroline mentioned sign supporting systems – namely Signalong and Makaton. Both these systems are compatible with the signs shown in *Teach Yourself Baby Signing* and Sing and Sign. These systems are designed for use *with* speech, and therefore the keyword approach to signing that is used throughout this book is entirely appropriate. Children with Down Syndrome may be advised to learn Makaton or another sign support system. A few signs may vary, and this is largely due to the dexterity of a small baby's hand. For further information on signing systems, please refer to Chapter 08 where this subject is covered in more detail.

Please note: Down Syndrome (which is the correct terminology) is commonly referred to as Down's Syndrome in British English.

Speech delay

It is known that approximately 5 to 10 per cent of children have a developmental disability that causes a delay in their speech and language development. As with other areas, it is often the parents who are the first to notice that their child is not developing their language skills at the same rate as similarly aged children and will describe their child as 'not talking', 'a late talker', or 'not speaking yet'. However, as we have already discovered in previous chapters, it is important to bear in mind that a child's language development involves more than just speech. It also includes other forms of communication, such as sign language, visual/pointing skills, and then as they get older, other skills such as writing.

What causes speech delay?

It is recognized that there are three main areas that can cause speech delay in children. These are problems with the:

- **output** of speech (anatomical problems with the vocal cords, etc.);
- **input** of speech (such as hearing loss)
- **processing** of speech (cognitive delay and developmental language disorders).

Alongside this, there are two main types of speech delay:

1 **Expressive** delay – which is the inability to generate speech.
2 **Receptive** delay – which is the inability to decode or understand the speech of others.

Of course some children may have a delay with a mix of both types, which is known as mixed expressive/receptive delay.

Some children with an expressive delay are just 'late talkers' and have a delay in their speech development. These children will develop normal speech and language skills as they get older without any treatment. Unfortunately, there is no way to differentiate children with this type of delay, who will have improvement of their speech without intervention, from those children who will require treatment. You can only tell in hindsight and it is not advisable to just 'wait and see' whether your child's speech will improve.

Most children with speech delays have developmental language disorders (DLD), with an inability to generate speech. This is known as expressive delay. The good news is that children with expressive delay will generally meet normal age-appropriate visual language skills, which could be recognizing parents and objects, responding to other's facial expressions, as well as following instructions that are accompanied with a gesture or sign indicating what you want done. These children will seem to have normal comprehension or understanding of other people's speech, and will generally be meeting all other normal age-appropriate auditory receptive skills (recognizing and turning toward sounds, following one- or two-step commands without a gesture, pointing to named body parts and objects). With early intervention of specialists and a good speech therapist, most of these children will have improved speech by the time they begin school and their speech will ultimately become normal.

Another important cause of speech delay is hearing problems, and so all children suspected of having a speech or language delay should have their hearing formally tested. This can be arranged through your GP or health visitor. It is not enough that you think your child hears because he responds to you when you call him from another room, or responds when he hears a dog bark, or you clap your hands. With my own son his hearing seemed to vary depending on the day, weather or type of sound. I had convinced myself he could hear fine (or it was just childhood selective hearing!). The fact was he had a significant hearing loss. It is important to let the experts check it out if you have any concerns.

There are other causes of speech delays, but things that *don't* cause speech delays are a child being 'tongue-tied', being 'lazy', having a lot of siblings that 'talk for him/her', or living in a bilingual family.

Perhaps a common misconception can be that if your child is already having problems talking, then signing will only inhibit them further. Maybe it is helpful to consider it another way: if you child is already having problems with speech, then how wonderful to provide them with the opportunity to be able to communicate. The frustration that a child with verbal language difficulties experiences can be huge – providing them with a way to effectively communicate can provide enormous relief.

Premature babies

A premature baby, or 'premie' as they are often affectionately called, is born before the 37th week of pregnancy. Premature birth occurs in between 8 to 10 per cent of all pregnancies in the UK. Because they are born too early, premies weigh much less than full-term babies. Premature infants are therefore prone to a number of health problems, mostly because their internal organs aren't completely ready to function on their own. The more mature your baby is at birth, the more likely it is that they will not have any medical problems.

When monitoring premature babies, careful attention is paid to the development of the nervous system, including the achievement of motor skills like smiling, sitting, and walking, as well as the positioning and tone of the muscles.

Speech and behavioural development are also important areas during follow-up. Some premature infants may require speech therapy or physical therapy as they grow up. Signing can prove a valuable part in aiding their development, as Katy found out in the following example.

> As a mum of an 8-week premature baby, I was worried about his development and despite knowing that his development at age 6 months was likely to be that of a 4-month-old, I didn't want it to because he had still been here for 6 months. Apart from being a great believer in baby signing, this was my sole reason for taking him to signing classes as I wanted to do anything I could to increase his chances of speaking early (well, when other babies his age did). It turned out that he said his first words, 'all gone', at age 13 months in the middle of a class when we put Jessie cat back in the box. Interestingly, 'all gone' was also his first sign at age 11 months after finishing his dinner. Now, at age 19 months, he can say anything he wants to, although the words he says regularly are words that we sign at classes and home.
>
> Katy Duckett

Deafness

Deafness comes in varying degrees, which are often described as mild, moderate, severe or profound. Hearing levels are often described in terms of decibels. During this section I have used the word 'deaf' to cover all types and degrees of hearing loss.

There are generally two types of deafness:

1 **Sensori-neural deafness,** or nerve deafness as it is sometimes called, is a hearing loss in the inner ear. This usually means that the cochlea in the inner ear is not working properly.

2 **Conductive deafness** means that sound cannot pass through the outer and middle ear into the inner ear. This is often caused by blockages such as wax in the outer ear, or fluid in the middle ear (glue ear – see page 124).

There are over 35,000 deaf children in the UK, with at least two deaf children being born each day. Of these children, 90 per cent are born to hearing parents with little experience of deafness. Very few deaf children have no useful hearing. Most deaf children can hear some sounds at certain frequencies and volumes, and with the use of hearing aids they are often able to hear more sounds.

My son was born 10 weeks early and, possibly due to him having to be resuscitated at birth, was born with a moderate/severe hearing loss. We didn't find out until he was 2, so we were so fortunate that we had decided to Sing and Sign with our baby before we knew we would come to rely on it as the only form of communication for quite a while! Joseph was delayed with the whole communication, not just speech and language and it took a few months to get his first sign – 'more' food! After that the signs flowed and then the speech arrived! Joseph is almost 5 now and as his speech is often unclear he will still sign to get his point across.

As Joseph is being brought up as a 'deaf child with speech' he didn't need to learn sign language, but knowing basic signs has helped him communicate with deaf children who sign, that we inevitably meet at deaf clubs etc. We were very aware that Sing and Sign used signs that were based on Makaton, but Makaton is based on BSL and most of the animals and suchlike are the same!

I cannot thank Sing and Sign enough for making signing fun, easy to learn and helping us through all those frustrating times that could have been so much worse without the communication that we had worked on!

I just wish I had signed with my first child who had no speech and language delays. I am positive it would have lessened those terrible twos tantrums! I will certainly be taking baby number 3 to classes.

Vicki Melville-Reed, mum to Jacob and Joseph

Deafness makes it harder for children to learn to communicate and many families face challenges in establishing communication with their deaf child. You will find some helpful tips at the end of this chapter on how to aid communication with a deaf child. Deaf children need to have access to fluent language so that they can develop good communication and language skills. This could either be through spoken language or sign language or both together. As Sing and Sign starts with babies as young as 6 months, many parents with deaf children have found it an invaluable resource, aiding communication with their child. Some will go on to learn the formal language for deaf people – BSL (British Sign Language) whilst others will use signing support systems, but a further explanation can be found in Chapter 08.

There is a huge amount of support available for deaf children; your GP, health visitor or local hospital should be able to point you in the right direction, and the National Deaf Children's Society is an invaluable resource for parents too (www.ndcs.org.uk).

My brother, Richard, is 17 months younger than me and is profoundly deaf. In the 1970s the 'experts' recommended that my parents use an oral/aural approach as 'signing would discourage speech'. As kids we communicated easily through lip-reading and our own gestural system, despite being told back then to 'sit on your hands'. Once at school, Richard quickly started to pick up signs from other children and he would share these with me. He continued in the oral system but it became more and more clear to us that the children from deaf families where signing was their first language, were the most sociable and rounded human beings; they were always involved in family discussions (where we had to remember to include Richard, as he would miss so much when we were just talking); they absorbed general knowledge from observing the conversations around them, just as hearing children overhear facts and opinions; they had a stronger sense of identity from being included, rather than always being on the periphery. My experience with my brother led me to decide to become a Teacher of the Deaf but in the 1980s this qualification didn't actually include sign language training! In 1992 I took my British Sign Language Stage 1 exam (and later my Stage 2) and went to work in a Total Communication school for deaf children. My brother now works in computer-aided design in an office full of hearing people with whom he communicates by email and lip-reading! But his social life is mostly within the deaf world where he is most comfortable with his own language, BSL.

Julie Warriner

Glue ear

Glue ear is a very common condition, with one in five children (especially pre-school children) suffering glue ear. This is also by far the most common cause of mild hearing loss in babies and children. Glue ear is essentially a build-up of sticky fluid behind the eardrum. The space behind the ear drum (middle ear) is normally full of air, allowing the drum to vibrate. Air gets into the middle ear through a tube which leads to the back of the nose, close to the adenoids. The tube opens when you swallow, yawn or blow your nose but it often doesn't work very well in children meaning that air cannot get into the middle ear, which fills up with fluid instead. This fluid 'glue' of glue ear is what causes mild to moderate hearing difficulty.

> *I decided to sign with Thomas because of my background as a Teacher of the Deaf and my knowledge of signing. Someone told me about the Sing and Sign video and that got me started! I had no idea at the time that Thomas would turn out to have hearing difficulties (glue ear) but I'm sure all the extra input from the signing has counteracted any possible language difficulties that may have arisen from the condition. As a baby Thomas had constant ear infections and burst eardrums. At 3 he is now being considered for grommets. He has also had a speech and language therapy assessment due to some difficulties with active nasal fricatives (v, b, f, s) which is all connected to his constant colds and breathing difficulties. Despite a few pronunciation problems and the fluctuating hearing, the Speech Therapist confirmed what I know: he has incredible language and vocabulary for a child who is not yet 4! I wholeheartedly believe that baby signing has given him the best possible start.*
>
> Julie Warriner

The most common cause of glue ear in children is congestion of the nose, causing blockage of the tubes, frequent colds/flu (which is why glue ear is particularly common in winter) or allergy/hay fever, sinusitis or recurrent ear infections. Smoking in the household is also known to be a contributing factor.

The good news is that glue ear can clear up of its own accord usually after a few weeks, although it *can* be months or sometimes years, but most will need no treatment. It is unusual after the age of 8 and seldom has any harmful long-term effect on the ears. It is only when the hearing loss is persistent and adversely affecting the child's speech, behaviour or education that treatment may be necessary – usually in the form of grommets.

Case study

As a family we were thrust into the realms of having a child with a significant hearing loss. As Josiah was our second child we were already in the habit of signing and so continued signing with him till his speech was well developed. He started signing very early, but maintained only a handful of signs till he was almost 14 months when he really took off – so different from our experiences with our first son who signed proficiently from 7 months! He seemed to speak quite early and had a very good comprehension of language.

At around 2½ years of age things were progressing well, and then he had an ear infection – our first and last. It did seem to affect his hearing, but that was only to be expected. It was a few months down the line when we started to notice that he still hadn't got his hearing back to normal, but by then we were more concerned about other areas of his behaviour. He had always been a very happy, contented child, growing into a lovely toddler responding well to people. His behaviour seemed to deteriorate rapidly. He was given over to mega temper tantrums and unexplained episodes of crying – he also went from being almost totally toilet trained to having to go back into nappies – it seemed like within a few short months, someone had transported my little boy.

During this time my best friend (who incidentally has a deaf child with moderate to severe hearing loss) questioned me over my son's hearing. To my shame I kept ignoring this, telling her he was fine. In reality there were times when he did seem to hear quite well and other times when he seemed to ignore you completely. My reasoning was that all children have 'selective deafness' especially when it is something they don't want to hear!

It was only when our health visitor contacted us to find out how things were going, that I mentioned he was still in nappies, behaviour was absolutely terrible, and that I wasn't sure he was hearing everything we were saying, however I still wasn't fully convinced as this seemed to fluctuate. He also had periods when he was crying at night and was getting more difficult to settle. I felt instead of growing and developing, in a short time my little boy was regressing, and by now his speech was affected. Certain words he used to pronounce clearly, we were now struggling with. We had naturally gone back to using signing a little more with him.

After a few questions the health visitor said she would like to refer him for a hearing test at the hospital. Surely if he had a hearing loss then it would be consistent? I have to say at this time, a good six months from his initial, and only, ear infection, I was beginning to struggle in my relationship with him. Everything I tried didn't really seem to work. He became more distant, sometimes in his own little world where you would feel like you were intruding. He was also becoming increasingly clumsy, falling over things – however on the whole, we struggled on, until the day of his hearing test.

Even at this point, I thought the hospital tests might find he had a mild hearing loss in one ear, but certainly not both. During the test he seemed unable to follow simple commands the audiologist asked of him. He explained that he thought he was just a little young for some of these tests. I assured him he was more than capable of those instructions. I therefore made Jos look at me (so natural with signing!) and using words and signs, told him what he needed to do – he did it perfectly! I told the audiologist that he obviously couldn't hear his commands, but he was incredibly capable. When it came to measuring the amount of air passing through the middle ear we were shocked to discover there wasn't any air passing through in either ear. In fact Jos was hearing at a very low level, being classed as moderately verging on severely deaf! I was so shocked! The consultation seemed to finish quite quickly and we were given several leaflets on glue ear. Following advice we asked about the 'speech banana', an easy reference guide to show what sort of sounds, consonants and vowels a child is hearing. Jos was only hearing about five letters.

Following this consultation I went through a range of emotions. Partly guilt from not pursing things further, amazement that I had informed other parents on these types of issues, urging them to seek professional advice, but been blind to it in my own son. I also felt incredibly protective of him, and relieved it was nothing too serious. I then, of course, wanted to do all I could for him in the intervening process. Although the initial diagnosis with regard to his hearing loss wasn't good, the overall outcome is normally excellent, with most children not having further problems after treatment.

We also went on to talk to his playgroup about how they could help him using more signs which we printed from the Sing and Sign website (www.singandsign.com) and making sure he was looking at them when giving instruction [see 'Aiding communication with a deaf child' below], we also received a referral for speech therapy. In addition to this, we went back to using many more signs with Jos. However, he was now 3 years old, and I had to learn new signs over and above the signs we had previously learnt with him as a young baby, as I now required additional signs that were developmentally appropriate for him.

Almost a year from his first infection he was booked in to have grommets fitted. This is quite a simple procedure and takes about half an hour, although it's never easy as a parent watching your child being anesthetised and going into theatre. Signing again was invaluable. Jos very clearly demonstrated to the nurses that he was not going to go onto the bed – any suggestion, and he clearly said and signed 'NO'!

The good news, as happens with many children who have glue ear, is that things immediately went back to normal, and I had my lovely little boy back again. Seven months on, however, we have noticed he again is not hearing words correctly, waking more at night, so we are off to visit the consultant again – we might need the next size up in grommets.

Symptoms of glue ear

- Fluctuating hearing loss.
- Brief episodes of earache, lasting two to three hours, often at night.
- Inability to listen or pay attention. Tendency to daydream.
- Behaviour problems/tantrums.
- Recurrent ear infections.
- Speech problems, especially in young children, usually mild. Difficulty in saying some of the quiet consonant sounds and in developing use of language generally.
- Poor balance.

Aiding communication with a deaf child or a child with hearing loss

Below are some points to remember when you are communicating with your child, or points to pass onto other caregivers. They are important because they give your child the best chance of understanding you. These apply to children who use either oral skills, such as speech and lip-reading, or use sign language, or to those children who use a combination of both:

- Make sure that you have your child's attention before starting to sign or speak to them.
- Maintain good eye contact and speak clearly and naturally – keeping your voice up, but don't shout! Ensure only one person is speaking at a time.
- Tell everyone involved with your child such as friends and family, playgroup, etc. about your child's condition, maybe using these helpful tips as a guide.
- If your child does not understand a word or sign, try to use a different one with the same meaning.
- Try to keep background noise to a minimum. Turn off the TV when talking. Sounds bounce off hard surfaces, which can make listening difficult for children with hearing aids or for those with mild deafness who don't use hearing aids or amplification devices.
- Although communication may have been difficult, do remember to talk a lot to your child about what you are doing, or what your child is doing or looking at.
- Try and use signs and gestures with appropriate facial expressions to support what you are saying – remember deaf children rely so much more on visual clues.
- Make sure your child knows when there is a new topic of conversation so that they understand the context.
- Be patient. Try not to get angry when your child keeps saying 'What?', 'Pardon' or 'Uhhh'.
- Take extra care when out and about with your child, especially around traffic – they may not be able to hear you clearly in a busy street.

07

signing with older children

In this chapter you will learn:
- how to use signs with emerging speech
- the benefits of signing and reading
- developmentally appropriate signs.

Getting ready for speech

Learning to talk is a long journey for children – they will understand more than they are able to say, and those early words can often be difficult to understand. You may not know if your child is saying 'buh' for ball, Barney, the preferred toy of the day, or even their favourite book. Signing can be fantastic in distinguishing what your child's ambiguous sounding word actually means, therefore enabling you to accurately decipher what it is they are wanting. It also remains an important opportunity for you to be able to correctly reinforce the spoken word. This obviously lessens frustration on both sides enormously and will therefore help increase your bond. Parents of signing children will often testify their children don't have temper tantrums from not being understood, they just have them for being told 'no' or not getting their own way!

Most children will follow very typical patterns of speech sound development, called phonological processes, which are a normal part of the speech development process. Some patterns can include sound or syllable substitutions, omissions or additions.

As we have discovered, a baby's first word tends to appear around their first birthday, with a more rapid growth at around 18 months of age. So children will often learn 'true words' mixed with jargon or 'babbling' to try and imitate the adult conversations they hear around them. For example, 'ahhh oooo' is unrecognizable as 'thank you'. However, your baby will pick up on the vowels and probably mimic the intonation and lilt in your voice, therefore distinguishing it from true 'baby babble', allowing it to be acknowledged as an attempt at 'thank you'. These early practice attempts at dialogue gradually develop into more intelligible speech.

Continually reinforcing signs with the spoken word really encourages children to start vocalizing the words they have been signing, until they drop the signs altogether in favour of speech. Speech naturally takes over as the main form of communication, so you shouldn't be worried that if your child begins signing they will never stop, or will continue and take the place of speech. If you are following guideline No. 3, 'Always say the word you are signing', your child will unsurprisingly begin to pronounce words and use their hands less.

> *At his 18-month check-up my son's speech and language development was very advanced for his years. We continued signing to him when he was learning his colours and phonics, even though his speech was very good, but obviously as soon as he could say certain words, the signs just naturally fell away.*
>
> Catherine with her son Michael

How signing facilitates speech development

Compared to 30 years ago, there is now far more evidence that signing can and does aid the development and facilitation of speech, dispelling an earlier myth that signing might actually inhibit speech. Signs act as a go-between while learning spoken words, when both are consistently paired in teaching. In addition, the neurologically based links between manual activity and speech suggest that there is a natural affinity between the two modes of communication. A study by Reid (1984) found that not only were signs learned more quickly than words, but that children who learned signs first, subsequently found it easier to learn words. They seemed to have developed an understanding of the principle of labelling in sign, which then transferred to the spoken word. Two other studies suggest that signing can directly facilitate articulatory skills, and that this effect may be due to the controlled movements of signing, providing a 'motor plan' for accompanying speech.

Very soon toddlers/older children move from signing their favourite word, to saying those very same words. It is in the early days, when speech is still immature, that signing will continue to enhance and facilitate communication.

It is great to keep encouraging this, and one way this can be achieved is by beginning to give them more choices. In the early stages, a generic sign for 'eat' was entirely appropriate for whatever food your baby liked. Now choices of favourite foods and drinks will be fun for your baby and for you. Would you like milk? Or maybe water? *Which* would you like: apple or banana? Baked beans or toast? Try using some of the signs provided below and on the accompanying CD to help you with some preferred foods. If you don't know, and you can't find the signs for your baby's favourite foods, then be prepared to be inventive and consistent with the signs you invent. Keep in mind that baby signing is a superb tool to help you and your baby understand and enjoy each other even more.

WHICH

How to sign it
Start as if you are signing 'areoplane' (fist, palm down and thumb and little finger sticking out) use thumb and forefinger to 'seesaw between choice'.

When to use it
As the action suggests, this is a great one to use when offering your child a choice – maybe they can't make up their mind which item of clothing to wear, or which piece of fruit to choose, use this sign when you are asking '*Which* one would you like?'

APPLE

How to sign it
Mime eating an apple.

BANANA

How to sign it
Mime opening a banana.

TOAST

How to sign it
Fingers together, palms facing you, pop both hands up as if they are toast popping out the toaster.

CAKE

How to sign it

One hand flat, palm down, the other hand (clawed) comes down on top, remaining clawed.

figure 45 cake

BISCUIT

How to sign it

One arm flat against your body, with hand up by opposite shoulder. With the other hand (fingers together), tap the elbow twice.

figure 46 biscuit

Speech sounds

In order to speak clearly, babies need to master a wide range of speech sounds – vowels, diphthongs and consonants. It is suggested that the signs help to differentiate speech sounds for babies and children, whose articulation can then improve considerably. So playing around with fun sounds can be a wonderful way to encourage the practice and awareness of the different sounds we use in speech. There are so many of them to master and some children can take a long time to say some of these sounds correctly.

Top tip

To help your child with speech sounds, play a game pulling various toys out of a bag – almost overemphasize the sound the toy or animal makes, i.e. mooooo for cow, neeeeowwww as in an airplane etc.

Use every opportunity to show your baby how to enjoy simple speech sounds and be assured that there is nothing wrong if, for the time being, your baby calls a clock a 'tick-tock'; an ambulance a 'nee-naw'; or a sheep a 'baa-baa'. Ideally you should repeat, 'yes a nee-naw, that's an ambulance, isn't it?' Anything that encourages vocalisation and enjoyment of communication is definitely a good thing!

A sign can be held static as a model to imitate. Hands can be moulded and shaped into signs far more easily than sounds can be shaped into words. (Grove 1986)

Sometimes babies charmingly and spontaneously use signs in combination, as their expressive capabilities are way ahead of their verbal skills. It is common for first-rate little signers to sign 'Where Daddy?' or 'Dog gone' etc. By giving babies an opportunity to 'name' objects at a very young age using signs, they soon have the ability to form such simple sentences. This often begins by using just signs, but may progress to use a combination of signs and words. Therein lies the temptation for you to begin signing longer sentences, using a few signs each time. However, baby signing does not intend to keep up with your baby in this explosion of grammatical achievement (unless, of course, you are keen for your baby to become bilingual in BSL, and would therefore need to enroll on an accredited course, or you are signing action songs). Typically, developing babies do not need to be shown signs in combination, or in fuller sentences, incorporating any grammatical structure. Everyday speech has a rhythm and a natural lilt. It is important for babies to pick up on this, as they are beginning to form small immature sentences of their own. It is amazing to think our pre-verbal babies can communicate in sentences. Below, Jo tells how her daughter uses a combination of signs to communicate before speech.

> *My daughter Jess is now 15 months old and signing in sentences. 'More' is her favourite sign, and very well used – 'more swing', 'more banana', 'more music', 'more swimming', 'more, more, more'! But she also has a great range of signs. Speech that cannot yet be clearly understood is made clearer by use of the appropriate sign at the same time, so the confusion between her desire to see her 'Nana' and to eat a 'banana' is becoming less frequent!*
>
> Jo and Jess from Bristol

> **REMEMBER:** Even if your child begins signing fuller sentences, you should still keep your signing simple and offer only one sign per sentence (unless, of course, you are signing action songs).

Reading a book together

It is never too early to read with your child – in fact, many libraries will actively encourage parents to sign up very young babies and use the vast resources they have on offer. Some of the best opportunities to enjoy signing with your baby come when you look at a book together. There are so many friendly and colourful books for babies, full of pictures that show everyday objects such as animals, vehicles, food, routines... lots to talk about, and objects that your baby may well know the sign for.

When your baby already knows and uses a few signs, you can both enjoy a book together, naming the pictures you see with the signs you know. From your baby's point of view, books become more of a shared experience, so rather than always being *read to*, your child has a wonderful opportunity to 'read' some pages to you. Many signing babies love to 'read' straight through picture books offering a sign for everything they see – they find it great fun.

Word of caution...

Obviously there are great benefits to introducing books early to your child. However, please be aware it is not the most ideal way for your baby to learn *new* signs. This is primarily because you are both enjoying looking at the pages rather than each other. This is why this topic has been included with signing with older toddlers/children, rather than earlier on in this book. On the other hand, your baby is highly likely to be off to a great start with a love of books if they are already a strong little signer.

Again it's important to remember the golden rules of baby signing: be relaxed and avoiding getting your baby to 'perform'. So don't put any pressure on your baby to sign words just because you know they can, as there will undoubtedly be times when your baby will want you to do all the work.

Phonics

You may think your 16-month+ baby is too young for the alphabet; however, you might be surprised to learn that your baby already has some building blocks in place for learning to read. Think about what your baby already understands so far about language – that words and signs are symbolic of individual things that they see, want and think about. This is now natural for them and being taken for granted. In the next few years the process will begin of recognizing different symbols on a page to represent these words.

Rather than teach the alphabet as 'Ay, bee, see, dee' it is more helpful to use what is known as the phonetic sounds – 'ahh, buh, cuh, duh'. This can help children identify initial letters of familiar words as they begin to come phonetically aware. It is important to pronounce the letters correctly so your baby knows how they actually sound in words. Some of them are voiced, for example 'b' would be pronounced 'buh' and 'd' would be pronounced 'duh', whereas 'f' and 'h' would be unvoiced, for example they would be the whispered consonants 'ffff' and 'huh'.

You will find early alphabet books are a great resource for learning phonics. If your child is competent in signing certain words consistently and/or is trying to say those same words, this is an opportune time to begin introducing first letter sounds. By showing them a sign for a letter sound, the visual clue can help them remember and identify it. This is the same as when they learned the early gestures (e.g. 'eat', 'drink', 'milk', 'more'). Your baby's brain will store the visual image of the sign along with the sound of the word – which in turn facilitates word retrieval and builds vocabulary. Using letter signs can build on understanding and awareness of individual phonemes, a major step towards reading and spelling.

I began signing with my daughter Amy when she was 6 weeks old. I had intended to start when she was born but just couldn't get my head together enough at first! She did her first sign at 11 months and had 25 signs before she said a word at 13 months. She is now just 2 years old and I still find signing such a help! Amy has more language than any of her peers and uses full sentences with tenses and pronouns. We are now working on her letters and being able to sign the sounds as well as say them has really helped. We have always signed people's names using the first letter and Amy began to make links between them herself by saying 'B...Becky, like B...Brian'. Now Amy can readily identify what sound any word begins with, and can sign and point to most letters of the alphabet. Signing has also really helped build Amy's confidence as she can communicate harder words to me that she can't pronounce very well. If she doesn't know the actual sign, then she will sign the first letter to cue me in and I can guess more easily! I firmly believe this has led to a happier life for all of us as she does not become frustrated. I would definitely recommend signing for all ages as I believe that anything that enhances communication can only be a good thing!

Zoe Desmier

At the time you are introducing phonics and first letter sounds to your child, you may find some of your story reading changes. Imagine your child has just seen a bird on the page and signed (and maybe tried to say) 'bird', as this is a word and sign they are familiar with. Your conversation may go something like this: 'Yes that's right it's a bird, bird starts with the letter 'Buh' (signing the letter B)'. You may find your child begins to mimic your sign as well as the sounds. Interactions such as these can continue; the car is another great place for learning new words and letter sounds. Even as your child progresses towards speech, or indeed is proficient in their speech, you may find on any given journey they will enjoy pointing out the many things they see – a train, the motorbike etc. You can confirm their effort, congratulating them on correct recognition, and use the opportunity to tell them that train begins with the letter 't'. This is such a straightforward way to introduce them to the concepts of reading and spelling. This game can progress from what a particular word starts with, to what it ends with, and then later, all the letters in between!

Parents of signing babies have commented on how observant they tend to be, growing into confident children who develop impressive memories enabling them to better concentrate on set tasks. These are often the crucial skills for starting the processing of reading. Alongside that, signing babies will often have improved fine motor skills and dexterity as a result of signing, which can only pave the way in assisting with their pencil control and writing skills later on.

Colours

For older babies who are used to grasping new words and concepts with accompanying gestures, the signs for colours can be fun and a terrific memory aid. Begin by pointing out the primary colours: red, yellow and blue. As Helen and Eloise discovered, beginning the day with deciding what colour to wear is a great way to introduce these simple signs.

> *Eloise has continued to sign although has dropped her favourites – the animals (with the exception of 'penguin') and has picked up on colours instead. We've had several signing conversations about what colour clothes she will wear and often she is insistent it has to be either pink or blue.*
>
> Helen Tillinghast

RED

How to sign it

Use the tip of your index finger to move across your lower lip.

Tip: Think of putting red lipstick on with your finger.

YELLOW

How to sign it

Hold your left hand up with palm facing out, fingers together, thumb apart. With the index finger of your other hand, touch the outside join of your left thumb and index finger twice.

Tip: Not only are you making a 'Y', this is actually the sign for the letter Y.

BLUE

How to sign it

Run your right index finger along the back of your left hand.

Tip: Think of running your finger along your blue vein.

GREEN

How to sign it

Hold one hand still, palm down, then with the other hand flat, palm up, move it over the back of the still hand.

figure 47 green

Tip: Do this as if scything grass.

Now our little boy is beginning to talk we are still finding signing useful, in fact, possibly even more so. He is learning his colours and because he can sign as he speaks we can tell, for example, whether he is saying 'yellow' (which otherwise sounds a lot like 'hello'), 'red' or 'green' (which sound the same when he says the words). I'm convinced signing has helped his vocabulary; at the very least it has reassured me that he understands words and recognizes pictures because he has been able to sign his recognition (e.g. when we read a book together, or seeing birds and animals in the garden or the park) for many months before he began to speak.

Jane Kirkby and Ben

ORANGE

How to sign it
With an open hand at the side of your mouth, close it tight.

TIP: Do this as if squeezing an orange with your hand.

PINK

How to sign it
Touch your cheek with the tip of your index finger, making a small stroke.

TIP: Think of applying blusher with your finger.

PURPLE

How to sign it
Make an 'O' shape with your index finger and thumb, brush this twice across the tip of the other index finger.

TIP: Think of miming the letter 'P'.

WHITE

How to sign it
Mime picking at your collar.

Tip: Think of white collar worker!

BROWN

How to sign it
With a flat hand, make small circles on the inside of the opposite wrist.

BLACK

How to sign it
With an inward facing fist, make a small circle on your cheek.

Weather

Looking out the window is enjoyable and talking about the weather becomes fun when your baby is enjoying these things for the first time. Snow is a glorious wonder that many will get excited about when they see and feel it for the first time; fog, wind and rain mean wellington boots and puddles... plenty for you to talk and sing about.

Talking about the weather can often seem a national past-time, but it provides you with a daily opportunity to introduce your child to new signs and a fresh understanding of the world around them. Using weather signs can often be incorporated into routines, or when you are talking about going out – 'We need to put our coat on because it's *raining*', or 'It's *sunny* today, we are going to wear our hats and go to the park'. These signs will often go hand in hand with the hot and cold signs which can be found on pages 73 and 74.

As you will often find, the signs are mimicking the word, thus making it so much easier for you to remember. Also bear in mind, it isn't always necessary to show your child the 'perfect' sign, demonstrated without flaw, but more important that you continue to communicate, to show them signs for the world about them, and to be consistent with any sign that you choose – even if you make one up yourself!

RAIN

How to sign it
Wiggling fingers mime rainfall – start high and come down.

SUN

How to sign it
Make a circle shape in the air.

SNOW

How to sign it
Like rain, but with your hands swirling down in front of your face.

WINDY

How to sign it
With palms facing you, 'fan' hands in front of your face.

Potty/toilet training

In Chapter 03 we briefly covered the 'clean' and 'dirty' signs within the routines section – using them as a prelude to potty training. Some parents will choose to begin training their children within a few weeks of birth whilst others will start putting their child on the potty once they can sit up unaided. We have included potty training signs within the chapter on signing with older children as the majority of parents wait until their toddler is ready, which can be as early as 18 months and up to around 3 years old. Whatever your method of training, you will find the following signs beneficial.

TOILET

How to sign

The middle finger crosses your body to make two small upward brushes high on the opposite collarbone.

figure 48 toilet/potty

When to use it

This sign can be used to indicate your child needs to go to the toilet, so therefore can be applied whether they use the toilet or potty. However, the next sign is an alternative potty sign, should you wish to distinguish between the two.

POTTY

How to sign it

With hands shoulder-width apart, mime putting a potty from one side to in front of you.

DRY

How to sign it

With one hand, fingers in towards your palm, your thumb rubs over nails of the other fingers (little finger first).

WET

How to sign it

Finger tips touch your lip and rub together (miming showing they have become 'wet').

figure 49 wet

SIT

How to sign it

Two flat hands, one on top of the other, move down once, miming sitting.

figure 50 sit

When should you stop signing?

This is a very common question amongst parents. Some people, having begun to learn a new way of communicating with their baby, are less than keen to drop the signs completely. This may well be true if you have a deaf friend or relative you wish to communicate more effectively with. Alternatively, you may have discovered that even simple signing with your child can be a great asset to further developing your relationship, simultaneously enhancing their learning and communication development. Many playgroups, schools and even churches will now use some form of Makaton or other speech supported signing system to reinforce audible commands, songs or familiar routines. Children learn best when all their senses are stimulated: audible, visual, sensory etc. as we touched upon in Chapter 05. Older children who have difficulty with spellings, or a list of facts to remember, will often find signing can really add that extra dimension to their learning and help reinforce what they are trying to learn. Families of children with ADHD and learning difficulties will often incorporate movement with learning as they know this can aid memory retention.

Parents have found it can become second nature to 'talk' with their hands as well as their voice. A major benefit to parents is the way they can communicate with their child in crowded places, or to bring particular emphasis to something without raising their voice. The most obvious example is catching one of your children jigging up and down, engrossed in something else – all you need to do is call their name, sign 'toilet' and 'now' and off they trot, accident avoided as well as any embarrassment to them in front of their friends. Another sign you may notice parents using in the park is the 'dangerous' sign. This is particularly useful if you are occupied with one child, and notice the other child somewhere where they shouldn't be. Again, calling their name and using the 'no' and 'dangerous' sign can be all that is required.

I have watched pre-schoolers using signs to emphasize a point: especially if they really want that second biscuit. It's amazing how often the word 'please' will be reinforced with the accompanying sign!

So don't feel just because your child has started speaking, and is making great strides in this area, that your hands need to stop 'talking' so much. You and your child will still get a lot of benefit and probably enjoy the process too.

Children with sign language skills are bringing something valuable and worthwhile into their community, as well as gaining the advantage of a second language. If you have enjoyed signing with your baby, maybe this will inspire you to learn BSL...you never know!

08

frequently asked questions

In this chapter you will learn:
- answers to the most common questions asked of signing teachers
- what to do if you are worried about your child's speech development
- differences between various signing systems
- ways to learn through Sing and Sign.

If my baby learns signs will he/she still learn to talk?

This has got to be the most common question that is asked. Yes, of course they will! Signs are never used *instead* of words and therefore your baby will be greatly encouraged to communicate verbally, and in no way discouraged. Baby signing is not a replacement for talking to your baby, in practice it encourages you to talk *more*! The use of gesture is a natural form of early communication and won't hinder the process of learning to talk – in fact it actually gives it a boost!

'Bye-bye' is often among the earliest words babies say. Think about how we all encourage babies to wave 'goodbye', recognizing they will enjoy this as well as helping to make them aware of an important concept. There seem to be four typical stages:

1 Your baby will first start to recognize and enjoy Mummy and Daddy waving goodbye.
2 Then your baby will start to imitate you when you wave (probably to great applause and family excitement!).
3 Your baby will soon start to wave spontaneously as you get ready to leave (this is when we would say the baby is 'signing').
4 Eventually your baby will say the words 'bye-bye!', while waving.

The waving has actually encouraged this baby to say the word because of the positive feedback and enjoyment of the sign. It is the same principle with other words and signs.

What happens to signs as a baby begins to speak?

Babies may use signs and immature speech together for a while. As speech improves, even the most enthusiastic little signers will soon start to drop their signs in favour of spoken words until they are no longer used. A toddler's immature speech will soon bloom into two- and three-word spoken combinations and overtake their single-word signing prowess.

There is much variation among babies in how they start to talk, and signing babies are no different in how this process is achieved. Some babies' first words are their signing words, such

as 'more', 'all gone', or 'car' for example. This is probably
because they have heard these words over and over and are used
to communicating them. Speaking them is the obvious next step,
however, you will probably find your baby begins to say some
words while simultaneously using the sign. If your baby starts
doing this, it is entirely appropriate for you to stop using these
signs consistently yourself.

It is worth continuing with the gestures for the longer, more
complex words like 'crocodile' or 'dinosaur' for a while though.
I can remember one such time when my almost 2 year-old was
asking where the **$@!* was. Despite repeated efforts at trying
to understand him, I eventually said 'Sign it for mummy' he then
signed 'hippopotamus' (a huge mouthful for any young child to
say and it was no wonder I couldn't understand what he was
trying to say). Hippo was a very recent acquisition he had been
given, and I was unfamiliar with his attempt at saying the word.
Signing again gave us the opportunity to effectively
communicate even though he was talking fairly fluently by then.

Sometimes a baby's first words may be those they do not yet
sign, or do not know the sign for – there seems to be no hard or
fast rule. You may even find that your baby has some favourite
signs which they will continue to use for a while even though
they can say many other more complex words. For my son,
'sorry' was one of those words that remained signed for a very
long time in our household in favour of being spoken. However,
this is a word that even some adults find hard to say! Sometimes
when babies have all but finished with their signs, some make a
reappearance when they are upset or tired, using the old
gestures as a way of emphasizing what they are trying to say –
shouting in sign!

My baby is taking a while to use signs

This is not unusual – consistency at home is usually the key but
some babies are just later to communicate than others. Put no
pressure on yourself or your baby. Your baby's desire to
communicate with you will be strong and your patience will be
rewarded. If your baby is taking a while to use signs, it really is
worth persevering. Remember, your baby is benefiting so much
from your signing input, and your baby will sign when they
have something to say. The key is to watch what your baby is
interested in, for my first son it was animals (and still is!). Try

not to emphasize 'parent pleasing' signs initially, such as 'please' and 'thank you', but rather watch what it is your baby is looking at, as these motivational signs are the ones that bring most success. If you feel impatient that your baby has not yet returned the signs you have been using, don't worry, and remember the journey towards speech is not a race. The joy and excitement of your child's first sign will make your patience worthwhile – I promise!

Could signing inhibit a baby's natural instinct to learn to talk?

You can reassure all who ask this common question that baby signing is beneficial to speech development. As we have already established, it is vital to *always* say the word as it is signed. In this way, you support and emphasize the spoken label and the sign is not a replacement for it. The use of gesture is a natural stage of early communication and the introduction of baby signing will inspire a baby to develop enhanced communication skills and will greatly expand their vocabulary.

Unfortunately, some people are of the erroneous opinion that frustration at being unable to adequately communicate is 'good for' babies and that it creates the urge to speak. This is a myth.

Extensive research has shown that children become better communicators when their early attempts at communication are understood and responded to, not when they are frustrated.

Marilyn Daniels PhD (Associate Professor of Speech Communication at Pennsylvania State University) says: 'Including sign language in the communication mix can eliminate the frustration both parent and child often experience as they attempt to comprehend each other. It fosters pleasant discourse, clarifies meaning and creates better understanding between them. With the keener understanding, there also comes an authentic grasp of content. Sign does not hinder language development in any way, rather it fosters it. It picks up on the natural visual acuity young children possess and uses it to the child's advantage.'

How can I encourage my child to sign to me more?

Although we have encouraged you to start with simple signs such as 'eat', 'drink', and 'milk', this is more for your benefit to enable you to get into the habit of signing to your baby, as they are early signs that you can use many times during the day. However, these are not always the first signs babies will use – maybe because we are generally good parents who know when our child is hungry or thirsty the majority of the time, or they are just offered it many times a day and therefore do not need to ask for it. Asking your child more open-ended questions using the 'What' sign (waggling your index finger from side to side) is really useful. Giving them a choice of toy for example – '*What* do you want? Bird or duck?' Or even something as simple as '*What* do you want? Play or food?' To begin with they may point and grab at the item they want, but consistently showing them the correct sign will reap you the rewards.

In Sing and Sign class an early sign for many of the babies is the 'Where' sign. This is primarily because we have a wonderful surprise box in which our Jessie Cat hides in. We begin singing 'Where oh where oh where is Jessie?' – The squeals of delight as once again Jessie pops out are just magical! However, it is a great motivational sign, and one they seem to pick up very easily. Don't forget, babies will sign what is important to them.

Are you worried about your child's speech?

Babies are different and there is wide variation in how each baby develops their speech and language skills, just as there is when each child learns to walk. However, certain milestones are typical, so if you are at all concerned about any aspect of your baby's speech or communication, talk it through with your Health Visitor or doctor, and they can refer your child to a speech and language therapist for advice. You can also make this referral yourself if necessary. Details of local speech and language therapy services can be found through the telephone directory, GP clinic or the library.

What are the different signing systems in use?

There are two main signing systems in use in the UK: British Sign Language (BSL) and Makaton (or systems based upon this).

BSL is a language in its own right, and is the main means of communication within the Deaf community, who are passionate about their language. When signing with BSL you often won't speak fluently whilst signing because their language has its own grammar. For example, if you want to say 'What is your name?' when using BSL you would sign, 'Name, you what?' There are some baby signing programmes within the UK who use BSL. It is very important to respect BSL as a separate language and if you wish to learn it, or intend to teach your baby to sign as a second language, it is essential to do so properly in an accredited course (Council for the Advancement of Communication with Deaf People, CACDP).

Makaton and other systems such as Signalong are 'sign supporting systems' which use signs or gestures to *support speech*; they are not an additional language like BSL. Makaton and Signalong are widely used in nurseries and schools with children who need help with communication. Signs are compatible with many used by BSL, but the approach is distinct as signs are only used to highlight key spoken words. The main aim when signing with your baby is to always encourage speech, and not to teach an alternative language.

Sing and Sign is based on widely used UK gesture systems such as Makaton, Say It and Sign It, Signalong and others based on BSL. These systems are designed for use *with* speech and are used by speech and language professionals as well as in nurseries and schools.

For parents who are already using different signs, it doesn't matter which signs you use (for example, many parents have seen the sign for 'more' in American Sign Language (ASL) on TV and have adopted that), it is the philosophy and approach that count. If your baby has already become familiar with certain signs, you do not need to alter them just to fit in with a different approach.

Help! I don't know the sign for...

Often when parents have started classes and are seeing the benefits of signing, they want to begin signing everything – from every toy, to every type of food. Remember, in the early stages, the key is simplicity. We would therefore recommend using the sign for 'eat' (using one hand, bunch your fingers together and tap a few times to your lips – saying the word 'eat') for breakfast, dinner, lunch etc., and not necessarily trying to sign, peas, potato or even butternut squash! 'Eat/food' is sufficient in the early stages with your baby. It is only with the older baby/toddler we would recommend giving many more choices with different food types. You will notice a lot more variety in the Sing and Sign Stage 2 DVD and classes giving them many more choices.

It isn't always important to sign *the* sign for a particular item – if you don't know it, and it isn't on the CD accompanying this book, then you may wish to be inventive. Being consistent with *a* sign is just as beneficial as using the correct sign. The list provided isn't exhaustive, but should offer you an excellent starting place. In the following example, Jane found with her son Ben that he did just that.

> Another benefit of signing for us is that because signing now comes so naturally to him, Ben makes up his own signs to communicate things that he can't manage to say. So far, he has 'invented' signs for glasses/spectacles, watering can, colouring and 'Bob the Builder'(!). It is this proactivity in communication which is, for me, one of the most valuable benefits of signing.
>
> Jane Kirby

Alternative ways to learn the Sing and Sign way

Teach Yourself Baby Signing is based on the Sing and Sign method of baby signing, and references within the book have indicated a variety of aspects to the programme. Below is a brief overview. For further information please go to **www.singandsign.com**.

In a class: You can attend a weekly Sing and Sign group with other parents and babies. These fun music groups are run across the country.

At home: The Sing and Sign video/DVD contains signed action songs and nursery rhymes. Sing and Sign is suitable for babies from 6 months, whilst 'More Sing and Sign' is suitable for toddlers aged 14 months+.

Online: Provides access to the extensive Member's dictionary of baby signs for parents who want to create their baby's own personlized signing resource. Ideal for printing off to share with family, friends or others who look after your baby when you can't be there. Also available is a baby signing discussion forum where you can share stories and get advice from teachers, experts and other parents.

signing dictionary

Below is a quick reference guide for all the signs covered in *Teach Yourself Baby Signing*. Many of these signs can also be found on the accompanying CD. Those marked with an asterisk (*) are ones that are illustrated in the book.

AEROPLANE – page 70

Make a fist and then have your thumb and little finger sticking out as if they are wings. You can then move your 'plane' through the sky, making the appropriate 'neeeooooowwww' sound!

ALL GONE/FINISHED – page 33*

Begin by holding your fists together with your palms facing inwards, then move your hands out so your hands are flat and facing down.

ANGRY – page 84*

Clawed hands, with palms facing you, make small movements alternating up and down.

ANIMALS – page 66

With palms facing down, mime 'prowling' hands going forward.

APPLE – page 133

Mime eating an apple.

AUNTIE – page 101

With index and middle finger bent and slightly apart, tap your chin.

BANANA – page 133*

Mime opening a banana.

BATH – page 60*

Cross your arms over your chest and mime washing yourself.

BED – page 63

Put your hands together on one side of your face, and then tilt your head – just as if your hands are becoming your pillow.

BEE – page 67

With your thumb and index finger together, make random loops in the air. Great with a good 'bzzzzzzz' sound too!

BIRD – page 67

With your thumb and index finger of one hand, open and close several times (keep the other three fingers clenched) – just as if you are doing a mime for opening and closing a birds beak.

BISCUIT – page 134*

One arm flat against your body, with hand up by opposite shoulder. With the other hand (fingers together), tap the elbow twice.

BLACK – page 142*

With an inward facing fist, make a small circle on your cheek.

BLUE – page 140

Run your right index finger along the back of your left hand.

BOAT – page 70*

Touch your finger tips together, palms facing inwards but apart, so you are making a boat's 'bow' shape. Move your boat shape forward.

BOOK – page 62

With both hands clasped together, mime opening a book.

BOY – page 99

Index finger sweeps under your chin from left to right.

BROTHER – page 99*

Make a fist, with thumbs up, knuckles inwards, rub up and down.

BROWN – page 142

With a flat hand, make small circles on the inside of the opposite wrist.

BUGGY – page 52

Mime pushing a buggy in front of you.

BUS – page 53

With arms parallel to your shoulders and straight arms, mime a big steering wheel.

CAKE – page 134

One hand flat, palm down, the other hand (clawed) comes down on top, remaining clawed.

CAR – pages 53 and 70

With hands in front of you and bent arms, mime a small steering wheel.

CAREFUL – page 79*

With your thumb and index finger form the letter 'c'. Move two 'c' shaped hands down and out from your eyes.

CAT – page 66*

With both hands making 'V' shapes with first two fingers, mime whiskers coming out from your nose.

CHICKEN – page 68

Your elbows become wings, so move them in and out, just like a chicken.

CLEAN – page 59*

Have one upturned faced palm, and then sweep your other open palm across it.

COAT – page 52

Mime pulling a coat around your shoulders.

COLD – page 74

Clench your fists directly in front of your chest, then in small movements shake them up and down, as if you were miming a 'Brrrr!'.

COUSIN – page 101

Make a 'C' shape with your thumb and forefinger, brush this twice under your chin.

CROCODILE – page 68

Think of your hands and arms as the jaws of a croc, so with both hands mime a big snapping action.

DADDY/FATHER – page 98

With closed index and middle finger tap twice on the closed index and middle finger of the opposite hand.

DANGEROUS – page 72***

Start with your index finger touching between your eyes; use a straight hand, facing sideways. Start between your eyes and move down strongly in an arc.

DIRTY – page 58***

Rub inside of wrists together, just as if you have dirty cuffs.

DOCTOR – page 90

With thumb and index finger, place on edge of wrist (as if taking a pulse).

DOG – page 66***

Index and third fingers of both hands move down once in front of your chest.

DOLL – page 64***

Hands in rocking position, but held still.

DRINK – page 29***

Drink is just like miming drinking from a beaker. Shape your hands as if you are holding a beaker and lift it a few times to your mouth.

DRY – page 144***

With one hand, fingers in towards your palm, your thumb rubs over nails of the other fingers (little finger first).

DUCK – page 68

A sign you may naturally do with your baby, but just as if your hand is a beak, open and close your whole hand as if your were making a 'quacking' move.

EAT – page 27*

Bunch your finger tips together and gently tap the corner of your mouth.

ELEPHANT – page 68

Make a fist, take it up to your nose and mime a big trunk, with a little flourish at the end.

FARM – page 50

Think of a farmer wearing braces. With both thumbs mime pulling braces forward.

FINISHED/ALL GONE – page 33*

Begin by holding your fists together with your palms facing inwards, then move your hands out so your hands are flat and facing down.

FISH – page 67*

Your hand faces sideways and mimes a fish tail movement 'swimming'.

FRIEND – page 101*

Clasp one hand with the other – as if shaking hands – mime this up and down.

FRIGHTENED – page 84

Clawed hand trembles in front of your chest.

FUNNY – page 83

Make a 'c' with index finger and thumb, and move up and down in front of your jaw, as if you are miming jaw moving up and down with laughter.

GENTLE – page 76*

With one hand, slowly and gently stroke the back of your other hand.

GIRL – page 99

Index finger makes two small strokes down from your cheek towards your mouth.

GOING OUT – page 49*

Cup your hand slightly, palm facing downwards, and mime 'going over the wall'.

GRANDAD/GRANDPA etc. – page 100*

With fingers spread apart, hand sideways, put the tip of your thumb on your forehead, and moving your hand forwards and down making small arcs in front of you.

GRANDMA/GRANNY etc. – page 100

With fingers spread, hand facing sideways, make small arc movements down from your chin.

GREEN – page 141*

Hold one hand still, palm down, then with the other hand flat, palm up, move it over the back of the still hand.

HAPPY – page 83*

Keep left cupped hand still, then rub right cupped hand from index finder out to thumb. Rub cupped hands with glee.

HAT – page 54

With a flat hand, put a 'hat' on your head, by patting your head.

HELP – page 42*

With outstretched arms, make the thumbs up sign with your right hand, put this hand on-top of your upturned left palm, then move both hands together towards your chest.

HOME – page 55*

Mime a roof, saying 'home' as your fingertips touch.

HOT – page 73*

With five fingers spread apart, quickly touch your fingers to your lips and then withdraw them.

HURRY UP – page 79

Index finger quickly strikes the side of the other index finger.

HURT – page 87*

With both index fingers pointing together – keep prodding them both together.

LAUGH – page 83

Make a 'c' with index finger and thumb, and move up and down in front of your jaw, as if you are miming jaw moving up and down with laughter.

LOOK – page 78

Use your index finger (as if pointing to your eye) then swiftly move it away in the direction of where you are indicating to your child to look.

LOVE – page 91

Two hands cross lovingly across your chest.

MEDICINE – page 90*

Make a loosely held fist with your left hand, then with little finger tip of your right hand trace around the top of the fist – as if tracing the opening of a small jar.

MILK – page 31*

Make a fist, then open and close your fist as if you are milking.

MONKEY – page 68

For this one, there is nothing for it but to look like a monkey, so with both arms stretched out horizontally, bend them at the elbow and start scratching under your arms!

MORE – page 28*

Make a fist with one hand, and then with the other hand flat, cover it over the top of the fist, just like you are pushing a cork into a bottle.

MUMMY/MOTHER – page 98

Index, middle and ring fingers tap twice on the opposite palm.

MUSIC (CLASS) – page 50

With index fingers in the air, wave from side to side as if conducting.

MUSLIN – page 64*

Make a fist, facing inwards, rub this up and down on your cheek.

NAPPY CHANGE – page 57*

Hold your fists together and twist from side to side.

NANNA/NANNY etc. – page 100

With fingers spread, hand facing sideways, make small arc movements down from your chin.

NAUGHTY – page 75

With a clenched fist in front of you, raise your little finger.

NO – page 44*

Use a flat hand facing away from your body, and make one movement starting in front of your body, taking your hand out to the side.

NOW – page 78*

Start with your palms facing upwards and your finger tips facing in at chest level, then make one strong movement down to waist level.

OPEN – page 43

Scrunch your hand up, and with a big flourish, open your fingers out.

ORANGE – page 141*

With an open hand at the side of your mouth, close it tight.

PAIN – page 87*

With both index fingers pointing together – keep prodding them both together.

PARK – page 50

With a flat hand facing downwards, make a wide circle from your waist.

PINK – page 141*

Touch your cheek with the tip of your index finger, making a small stroke.

PLAY – page 80*

With flat hands, make small upward moving circles in front of you, rotating your wrists.

PLEASE – page 92*

With a flat hand on your chin, finger tips pointing up, palm towards you, move your hand out and down from your chin in a large arc.

POTTY – page 144

With hands shoulder-width apart, mime putting a potty from one side to in front of you.

PURPLE – page 141

Make an 'O' shape with your index finger and thumb, brush this twice across the tip of the other index finger.

QUICK – page 79

Index finger quickly strikes the side of the other index finger.

RABBIT – page 68

With your index and middle fingers make 'rabbit ears' on your head, just twitch them forward slightly.

RAIN – page 142*

Wiggling fingers mime rainfall start high and coming down.

RED – page 140*

Use the tip of your index finger to move across your lower lip.

SAD – page 83

Flat hand (facing sideways, fingertips up) moves down the middle of your face.

SAND – page 51*

Think of rubbing flour through your fingers, do this action whilst raising your hands upwards.

SHARE – page 95*

Mime 'give' and 'take' with both hands, palms faced upwards.

SHEEP – page 68

With your little fingers, mime curly horns coming out from your temples.

SHOES – page 52*

With one hand, make a 'bridge' and mime putting a 'shoe' on the other hand.

SHOPS – page 49

With two hands starting close to your chest, mime pushing a trolley, so extend and 'push' your arms in front.

SISTER – page 99

Hooked index finger taps the bridge of your nose twice.

SIT – page 145*

Two flat hands, one on top of the other, move down once, miming sitting.

SLIDE – page 51

Flat hand mimes sliding down.

SNOW – page 143

Like rain, but with your hands swirling down in front of your face.

SORRY – page 94*

Make a fist, and rub small circle in the middle of your chest.

SUN – page 143*

Make a circle shape in the air.

SWIMMING POOL – page 49

Mime doing breast stroke.

SWINGS – page 50*

Two hands mime a swing action by your sides.

TEETH (Brush teeth) – page 62

Very simply, with your index finger, mime brushing your front teeth.

TEDDY – page 63*

Gently clawed hands cross, and hands tap your shoulders – almost as if you are making a cuddle gesture.

THANK YOU – page 93*

With a flat hand on your chin, finger tips pointing up, palm towards you. Move your finger tips out and down from your chin in a small static movement that should finish about 10–15cm from your face.

TIRED – pages 62 and 83

Clench your fist and rub your eye.

TOAST – page 134*

Fingers together, palms facing you, pop both hands up as if they are toast popping out the toaster.

TOILET – page 144*

The middle finger crosses your body to make two small upward brushes high on the opposite collarbone.

TOYS – page 80*

With flat hands, make small upward moving circles in front of you, rotating your wrists.

TRAIN – page 69*

With arms bent and fists clenched at your sides, mime train wheels.

UNCLE – page 101

Index finger brushes back of other little finger twice.

UPSTAIRS – page 61

Let your first and middle fingers of one hand make a walking movement 'up' invisible stairs.

WAIT – page 96*

Put both hands in front of your body, hands flat, palms outwards, move your hands purposefully down in front of you.

WET – page 145*

Finger tips touch your lip and rub together (miming showing they have become 'wet').

WHAT – page 77

Wave your index finger from side to side.

WHERE – page 40*

Hold your hands in front of you with palms facing upwards, making small circles.

WHICH – page 133

Start as if you are signing 'areoplane' (fist, palm down and thumb and little finger sticking out) use thumb and forefinger to 'seesaw between choice'.

WHITE – page 141

Mime picking at your collar.

WINDY – page 143

With palms facing you, 'fan' hands in front of your face.

YELLOW – page 140

Hold your left hand up with palm facing out, fingers together, thumb apart. With the index finger of your other hand, touch the outside join of your left thumb and index finger twice.

YES – page 47*

Make a fist with your right hand and 'nod' yes (from your wrist) with your hand.

index

teach
yourself ®

From Advanced Sudoku to Zulu, you'll find everything you need in the **teach yourself** range, in books, on CD and on DVD.

Visit **www.teachyourself.co.uk** for more details.

Advanced Sudoku and Kakuro	Beginner's French
Afrikaans	Beginner's German
Alexander Technique	Beginner's Greek
Algebra	Beginner's Greek Script
Ancient Greek	Beginner's Hindi
Applied Psychology	Beginner's Hindi Script
Arabic	Beginner's Italian
Arabic Conversation	Beginner's Japanese
Aromatherapy	Beginner's Japanese Script
Art History	Beginner's Latin
Astrology	Beginner's Mandarin Chinese
Astronomy	Beginner's Portuguese
AutoCAD 2004	Beginner's Russian
AutoCAD 2007	Beginner's Russian Script
Ayurveda	Beginner's Spanish
Baby Massage and Yoga	Beginner's Turkish
Baby Signing	Beginner's Urdu Script
Baby Sleep	Bengali
Bach Flower Remedies	Better Bridge
Backgammon	Better Chess
Ballroom Dancing	Better Driving
Basic Accounting	Better Handwriting
Basic Computer Skills	Biblical Hebrew
Basic Mathematics	Biology
Beauty	Birdwatching
Beekeeping	Blogging
Beginner's Arabic Script	Body Language
Beginner's Chinese Script	Book Keeping
Beginner's Dutch	Brazilian Portuguese

Bridge
British Citizenship Test, The
British Empire, The
British Monarchy from Henry
    VIII, The
Buddhism
Bulgarian
Bulgarian Conversation
Business French
Business Plans
Business Spanish
Business Studies
C++
Calculus
Calligraphy
Cantonese
Caravanning
Car Buying and Maintenance
Card Games
Catalan
Chess
Chi Kung
Chinese Medicine
Christianity
Classical Music
Coaching
Cold War, The
Collecting
Computing for the Over 50s
Consulting
Copywriting
Correct English
Counselling
Creative Writing
Cricket
Croatian
Crystal Healing
CVs
Czech
Danish
Decluttering
Desktop Publishing
Detox
Digital Home Movie Making
Digital Photography
Dog Training
Drawing

Dream Interpretation
Dutch
Dutch Conversation
Dutch Dictionary
Dutch Grammar
Eastern Philosophy
Electronics
English as a Foreign Language
English Grammar
English Grammar as a Foreign
    Language
Entrepreneurship
Estonian
Ethics
Excel 2003
Feng Shui
Film Making
Film Studies
Finance for Non-Financial
    Managers
Finnish
First World War, The
Fitness
Flash 8
Flash MX
Flexible Working
Flirting
Flower Arranging
Franchising
French
French Conversation
French Dictionary
French for Homebuyers
French Grammar
French Phrasebook
French Starter Kit
French Verbs
French Vocabulary
Freud
Gaelic
Gaelic Conversation
Gaelic Dictionary
Gardening
Genetics
Geology
German
German Conversation

German Grammar
German Phrasebook
German Starter Kit
German Vocabulary
Globalization
Go
Golf
Good Study Skills
Great Sex
Green Parenting
Greek
Greek Conversation
Greek Phrasebook
Growing Your Business
Guitar
Gulf Arabic
Hand Reflexology
Hausa
Herbal Medicine
Hieroglyphics
Hindi
Hindi Conversation
Hinduism
History of Ireland, The
Home PC Maintenance and
  Networking
How to DJ
How to Run a Marathon
How to Win at Casino Games
How to Win at Horse Racing
How to Win at Online Gambling
How to Win at Poker
How to Write a Blockbuster
Human Anatomy & Physiology
Hungarian
Icelandic
Improve Your French
Improve Your German
Improve Your Italian
Improve Your Spanish
Improving Your Employability
Indian Head Massage
Indonesian
Instant French
Instant German
Instant Greek
Instant Italian

Instant Japanese
Instant Portuguese
Instant Russian
Instant Spanish
Internet, The
Irish
Irish Conversation
Irish Grammar
Islam
Israeli-Palestinian Conflict, The
Italian
Italian Conversation
Italian for Homebuyers
Italian Grammar
Italian Phrasebook
Italian Starter Kit
Italian Verbs
Italian Vocabulary
Japanese
Japanese Conversation
Java
JavaScript
Jazz
Jewellery Making
Judaism
Jung
Kama Sutra, The
Keeping Aquarium Fish
Keeping Pigs
Keeping Poultry
Keeping a Rabbit
Knitting
Korean
Latin
Latin American Spanish
Latin Dictionary
Latin Grammar
Letter Writing Skills
Life at 50: For Men
Life at 50: For Women
Life Coaching
Linguistics
LINUX
Lithuanian
Magic
Mahjong
Malay

Managing Stress
Managing Your Own Career
Mandarin Chinese
Mandarin Chinese Conversation
Marketing
Marx
Massage
Mathematics
Meditation
Middle East Since 1945, The
Modern China
Modern Hebrew
Modern Persian
Mosaics
Music Theory
Mussolini's Italy
Nazi Germany
Negotiating
Nepali
New Testament Greek
NLP
Norwegian
Norwegian Conversation
Old English
One-Day French
One-Day French – the DVD
One-Day German
One-Day Greek
One-Day Italian
One-Day Polish
One-Day Portuguese
One-Day Spanish
One-Day Spanish – the DVD
One-Day Turkish
Origami
Owning a Cat
Owning a Horse
Panjabi
PC Networking for Small
  Businesses
Personal Safety and Self
  Defence
Philosophy
Philosophy of Mind
Philosophy of Religion
Phone French
Phone German

Phone Italian
Phone Japanese
Phone Mandarin Chinese
Phone Spanish
Photography
Photoshop
PHP with MySQL
Physics
Piano
Pilates
Planning Your Wedding
Polish
Polish Conversation
Politics
Portuguese
Portuguese Conversation
Portuguese for Homebuyers
Portuguese Grammar
Portuguese Phrasebook
Postmodernism
Pottery
PowerPoint 2003
PR
Project Management
Psychology
Quick Fix French Grammar
Quick Fix German Grammar
Quick Fix Italian Grammar
Quick Fix Spanish Grammar
Quick Fix: Access 2002
Quick Fix: Excel 2000
Quick Fix: Excel 2002
Quick Fix: HTML
Quick Fix: Windows XP
Quick Fix: Word
Quilting
Recruitment
Reflexology
Reiki
Relaxation
Retaining Staff
Romanian
Running Your Own Business
Russian
Russian Conversation
Russian Grammar
Sage Line 50

Sanskrit
Screenwriting
Second World War, The
Serbian
Setting Up a Small Business
Shorthand Pitman 2000
Sikhism
Singing
Slovene
Small Business Accounting
Small Business Health Check
Songwriting
Spanish
Spanish Conversation
Spanish Dictionary
Spanish for Homebuyers
Spanish Grammar
Spanish Phrasebook
Spanish Starter Kit
Spanish Verbs
Spanish Vocabulary
Speaking On Special Occasions
Speed Reading
Stalin's Russia
Stand Up Comedy
Statistics
Stop Smoking
Sudoku
Swahili
Swahili Dictionary
Swedish
Swedish Conversation
Tagalog
Tai Chi
Tantric Sex
Tap Dancing
Teaching English as a Foreign
   Language
Teams & Team Working
Thai
Thai Conversation
Theatre
Time Management
Tracing Your Family History
Training
Travel Writing

Trigonometry
Turkish
Turkish Conversation
Twentieth Century USA
Typing
Ukrainian
Understanding Tax for Small
   Businesses
Understanding Terrorism
Urdu
Vietnamese
Visual Basic
Volcanoes, Earthquakes and
   Tsunamis
Watercolour Painting
Weight Control through Diet &
   Exercise
Welsh
Welsh Conversation
Welsh Dictionary
Welsh Grammar
Wills & Probate
Windows XP
Wine Tasting
Winning at Job Interviews
Word 2003
World Faiths
Writing Crime Fiction
Writing for Children
Writing for Magazines
Writing a Novel
Writing a Play
Writing Poetry
Xhosa
Yiddish
Yoga
Your Wedding
Zen
Zulu

teach
yourself

baby sleep
andrea grace

Baby Sleep is a practical and sympathetic guide to overcoming night-time (and daytime) traumas. It will help you to devise a sleep plan that works for both you and your child, and is full of sensible advice to help parents and families put this difficult time behind them.

Andrea Grace is a health visitor, mother of four and sleep specialist whose clinic has helped many families to overcome sleeping problems with babies and young children – www.andreagrace.co.uk.